Praise for

This Is Mexico

"Carol Merchasin writes about San Miguel de Allende with affection and self-effacing wit, even as she mulls the contradictions and imperfections of her adopted country. *This Is Mexico* is wise and funny and true."

—Gerard Helferich, author of
Theodore Roosevelt and the Assassin

"*This Is Mexico* is one more thing to celebrate about living south of the border. Written with wit and humor, rich with insight and incident, it tells the story of one couple's journey into expat life, with all its accommodations. It is authoritative, yet intimate and personal, and blessed with humanity throughout. A valuable addition to expat literature, it is dependably interesting from start to finish."

—John Scherber, author of *Living in San Miguel*

"In the good-hearted tradition of Jack Smith's classic of the gringo-in-Mexico memoir, God and Mr. Gómez, Merchasin's *This Is Mexico* recounts a 'recovering lawyer's' adventures and many lessons in learning to live south of the border."

—C.M. Mayo, author of
Metaphysical Odyssey into the Mexican Revolution

"I am enchanted with Merchasin's description of Mexico. I have lived seventy of my ninety-four years in Mexico and still wonder whether the plumber's reply of *'Mañana'* to the question, 'When can you fix it?' means day after tomorrow, next week, or call another plumber. She captures the chaos, the music, and the pure joy of living here."

—Kathryn Blair, author of *In the Shadow of the Angel*

"A warm, witty, and lively recounting of settling into life in San Miguel."

—Tony Cohan, author of *On Mexican Time* and *Mexican Days*

"Merchasin's essays about Mexico nail the people, the culture, the experience of living here, the tender relationships. Some essays are poignant, some are funny, all of them are beautifully written and carefully crafted. I want to give this book to all my friends who wonder why I live in Mexico. The essays are accurate, nuanced, entertaining, enlightening. The writing is elegant and ranges from touching to hilarious. If you have any interest in Mexico, don't miss this book."

—Susan Page, Director of the San Miguel Writers' Conference and Literary Festival

"With writing that's as persuasive as a legal brief and as funny as your favorite relative's best stories, Merchasin captures the daily confusion of living in Mexico, a country filled with local characters reminiscent of Peter Mayle's rustic French neighbors. Smart. Witty. Warm. Engaging and enlightening, this is a brilliant gem of a memoir."

—Mark Saunders, author of *Nobody Knows the Spanish I Speak*

"In her touching memoir, Merchasin has captured the colors and chaos, the tastes and the trials that make up life in the city of San Miguel de Allende. In a refreshingly honest voice, Merchasin shows how weapons became fireworks and dangers morphed into kindness. She isn't afraid to show her naivety at the culture she finds, nor her surprise at how it comes to seduce her. Indeed, her candor is what makes this memoir unique. In her beguiling way, Merchasin draws us into a country open to life, and a people who opened to her, as she did to them."

—Mary Morris, author of *Nothing to Declare*

THIS IS
MEXICO

Published 2015
Printed in the United States of America
ISBN: 978-1-63152-962-7
Library of Congress Control Number: 2014956081

Book design by Stacey Aaronson

For information, address:
She Writes Press
1563 Solano Ave #546
Berkeley, CA 94707

THIS IS MEXICO

TALES OF CULTURE
AND
OTHER COMPLICATIONS

BY CAROL M. MERCHASIN

To Robert, whose fearlessness brought us to Mexico.
To Mexico, whose great heart kept us here.

TABLE OF CONTENTS

PREFACE

"There's one frontier we only dare to cross at night," the old gringo said. "The frontier of our differences with others, of our battles with ourselves . . . . I'm afraid that each of us carries the real frontier inside."

—Carlos Fuentes, *The Old Gringo*

I MOVED TO SAN MIGUEL de Allende, a town in central Mexico, in 2006. Even before the overwhelming US press coverage of drug violence began, people wondered about that decision. I did not have work here; I was a lawyer and independent consultant on employment law training issues. I could have lived anywhere.

People often asked me incredulously, "How did you get to Mexico?" If I felt flippant, I replied, "I turned left at Laredo." If I was honest, I said, "I'm not sure." Perhaps, like Carlos Fuentes' old gringo, I wanted to cross some different frontiers.

Whatever the reasons, soon I was writing tales of discovery. I sent them to family and friends, recounting stories of the often magical and mysterious, sometimes heartrending, workings of everyday life in Mexico. From health care encounters to pilgrimages, from the absurdities of the telenovela to the cultural subtleties of the language, I wanted people to see the joys and sorrows of life in this much misunderstood and often maligned culture. At the beginning of this cultural journey, I often said, "Well, yes, I suppose this *is* Mexico." Or, "For heavens sake, yes, I know this is *Mexico*, but . . ." Eventually, I arrived at my destination. "Yes, thank goodness, this is Mexico." Eventually, e-mails became stories, stories became essays, and *This is Mexico* was born.

It is estimated that almost one million Americans live in Mexico, while another twenty-one million travel and vacation here. Forty million US baby boomers between the ages of fifty-five and sixty-five may be looking to live in Mexico—its proximity to the United States, moderate climate, and lower cost of living are appealing. But often, our images of Mexico are limited to beach resorts, a *campesino* sleeping under a cactus, or beheadings by the drug cartel. While all of these images exist, they are not the whole story. Not by a long shot.

Mexico is a country of contradictions, a place where the past is alive in the present. As fellow inhabitants of the continent known as North America, we often fall back on the idea that Mexico is a country somewhat foreign but not exactly—a less developed version of the United States.

As Alan Riding, author of *Distant Neighbors: A Portrait of the Mexicans* said, "Probably nowhere in the world do two countries as different as Mexico and the United States live side by side." And yet our understanding of these differences is almost nonexistent.

I have changed the names of certain people to protect their privacy, but the stories I tell here are true to the best of my understanding and my ability to tell them. The statistics I have used in discussing crime and poverty are accurate as far as they go, but as we know, "there are . . . lies, damned lies, and statistics." My purpose in using them is simply to establish some comparative reference points, not an absolute truth.

This is Mexico is not a history book or a cultural treatise. It is my attempt to understand and explain the improbable events and small moments of a life in Mexico; to share the shards of bewilderment, misunderstanding, and frustration that have been cemented into a mosaic of love and appreciation.

I am not a historian, psychologist, anthropologist, or economist—I have no credentials except those open to us all. I write in the hope that you will celebrate Mexico with me and that you will deepen your understanding of what an extraordinary culture we have on, and within, our borders.

SECTION ONE

ONE WILD AND PRECIOUS LIFE

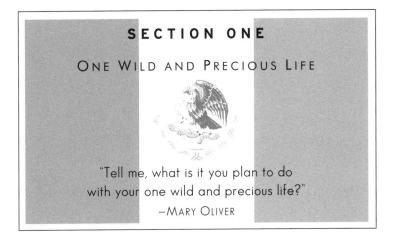

"Tell me, what is it you plan to do
with your one wild and precious life?"
—MARY OLIVER

Where We Wake Up
to the Revolution and Meet
El Circo Más Grande y Muy Famoso

————————

THE BOOM OF HEAVY artillery woke us at 5:45 a.m. on Wednesday, the day before Thanksgiving 2005. As it reverberated through our room at the Casa Luna, a charming bed-and-breakfast in San Miguel de Allende, Mexico, I shot out of the covers, my blood running cold, the metallic taste of fear in my mouth. My husband, Robert, sat up heavy with sleep and a questioning look.

"What was that?"

"I don't know—it sounded like heavy gunfire."

Silence. The night shadows were lifting, outlining rooftops in a gray, woolly light, but it was still too dark to see.

Boom. Boom, boom. The repeats echoed and bounced around, like a giant playing a pinball machine. I was terrified.

I should have focused more on the political situation in Mexico before I exchanged my frequent-flier miles for round-trip tickets to Mexico from Philadelphia. My mind scrambled into emergency-evacuation mode. Moving here was now out of the question.

THE DECISION TO MOVE to a foreign country is not one to be made over margaritas in an upscale Mexican restaurant in the United States, but that was how my husband, Robert, and I did it.

"*¿Música, señor?*" The mariachis came around to our table on our nod of assent. The violins entreated the trumpets in a spirited rendition of "De Colores," the only song we knew to ask for in Spanish.

"*Guacamole, señora?*" Soon the avocados were being hand ground in a lava-rock mortar and pestle at our table, their smooth, creamy green a counterpoint to lipstick-red tomatoes and snowy onions.

"Well," said Robert, "where shall we go?"

I looked up at the tufted piñatas swinging from the ceiling. I took in the musicians, now at another table.

"How about Mexico?"

Taking a piece of paper and a fountain pen from my well-worn briefcase stuffed with legal papers, I made two neat columns labeled "Pros" and "Cons." After the enchiladas with *salsa verde*, I pushed up the sleeves of my sweater and we got down to business. By the time the flan came, we were living in Mexico. *Where* in that vast landscape remained the only question.

LIFE IN A FOREIGN COUNTRY had long been lodged in my dreams. For three years in the 1960s, I lived in a village near Athens, Greece—a place of dirt roads winding to the sea, of community markets and men who pushed wooden carts through the lanes selling vegetables. The morning air was redolent of something previously unknown to me, a combination of spring, optimism, and wild oregano. No telephone (this was a now-unimaginable pre-cell phone era), no television, no oven, no washer, no dryer—it was my first experience of "no" creating "yes," less being more, the simplicity of fewer things and more delight in life.

In 1983, I visited Mexico, a country as open to life as I had found Greece, a place filled with people who sang impossibly sad songs and danced in their plazas, their air warmed by a southern sun. I loved the chaos, the exuberance of color, that smell I still smelled from forty-five years earlier—a combination of spring, optimism and, in this case, corn tortillas.

But Mexico was not in my immediate future. A late entrant in the sweepstakes of professional life, I went to law school at forty and on to a succession of large law firms at forty-three. I was making up for lost time, for unfunded IRAs and 401(k)s, the alphabet soup of initialed retirement-savings devices designed for the aging US population. Although I often felt like a hapless hamster on a turning wheel, I found it difficult to let go. But the day came when it was no longer worth the amount of life I had to pay for it.

Retiring would mean financial and psychological adjustments, but Mexico fulfilled that longtime yearning for foreign living. We knew exactly what we wanted from Mexico. We wanted to be where we could wake up to life, where we would not just walk down the street but walk down the street with light and air and color that was not available in Philadelphia, with people who looked different, with donkeys loaded with kindling and bags of cement—and we would do it in Spanish. We wanted a fresh perspective, to be engaged by life somewhere other than in a shopping mall or a traffic jam, to smell sunshine and grilling meat on the street. All of that—and Internet access.

Many people were skeptical of our plans.

"Mexico?" a coworker questioned, frowning. "Why Mexico? It's so backward."

"Why not France?" another suggested helpfully. "Somewhere with some culture?"

"Where in Mexico?" people asked, knowing only the beach resorts—Puerto Vallarta, Mazatlán, Cancún—as places suitable for living, as if Mexico had the Pacific Ocean and the Caribbean Sea and nothing in between.

"Isn't it too dangerous to live there?" Usually these comments were from people in nearby suburbs who found it too threatening to live in Philadelphia. I ignored them.

"What will you do?" they asked.

I didn't try to explain the smells, the color, the chaos. Mostly I smiled like a person who realized she was probably crazy and moved on. But "What will you do?" was a good question. Just short of sixty, I felt too young to give up work. We didn't aspire to retire; rather, we hoped to shift into fifth gear, a smoother drive for the long haul, where we would not be the cogs in other people's wheels. We would take the gold of our years of work and turn it into a simpler life. We would leave behind what didn't matter anymore to find what did.

We did not think about what Mexico wanted from us. But in a secret place in my mind that could not be seen and would not be heard from for a while lay the assumption that our being citizens of the United States of America, an advanced nation, meant Mexicans would learn from us and say, "How clever and advanced they are! We want to be like them." We couldn't have been more wrong.

Our idea that Mexico was a country adjoining the United States, and therefore not completely foreign, was also wrong. We had no sense that we were wading into cultural waters so deep that we would need more than a life preserver to stay afloat.

No. We learned all of that much later.

JUST THREE DAYS BEFORE, the midafternoon heat had risen to embrace us as we stepped onto the tarmac at the León airport. The terminal gleamed—shiny and more modern than I had expected. Our Mexican driver met us, a short, rugged man who spoke no English. He would drive us to San Miguel, our home base for the next ten days, well known for its temperate climate and sixteenth-century Spanish architecture. From there we would decide what to see, where to go, and how to clear a path to a life in Mexico.

Robert rode in the front seat because his Spanish was more adventurous than mine. I absorbed the bright heat and the high-desert landscape from the back. The glare of the afternoon sun shimmered on vast industrial complexes fading to dry fields, short, flat-topped trees, and unfinished houses, their empty windows gaping like missing teeth. We left the billboards and traffic of León, passing the occasional donkey, as we made our way up and over a mountain pass.

"Is that San Miguel?" I leaned forward and pointed into the distance, where a church spire stretched skyward and domed buildings nestled in the bottom of a bowl of gray-green hills. Bright Mexican colors glowed like a distant cubist painting.

"*Así es,*" he replied. It was.

San Miguel is not a quiet town. We discovered every activity had its own sound, creating a uniquely Mexican musical ballad to life. Bells chimed the time in fifteen-minute increments, others summoned the faithful with a first, second, and last call to Mass. Men who filled the gas tanks perched on flat roofs communicated with whistles, the low-tech equivalent of walkie-talkies. A man striking an iron bar, the metal against metal deafening, announced slow-moving trash trucks.

A man plied the streets, carrying buckets of peanuts and singing "*Cacahuates*" a cappella. Circus wagons added to the cacophony, their trucks—loudspeakers tied to the roofs—circling narrow streets with caged lions, tigers, and ostriches, inviting us to come and see *El Circo Más Grande y Muy Famoso*. Although with three trucks and one tent, I doubted it was indeed the largest and most famous.

The clamor of the evening reverberated as we strolled down cramped sidewalks to the Jardín, the main square and historic center of the town, which was established by the Spaniards in 1542. Children were coming home from school: giggling, gossiping girls, arm in arm in the middle of cobblestone lanes; boys running and shouting. The blast of the mariachis' trumpets rounded the corner as we did, heralding the sight we had come to Mexico to see— musicians; food vendors with steaming carts; arched colonnades; people everywhere, sitting on benches, at café tables, and perambulating the perimeter of meticulously pruned trees. A salmon-pink limestone church, so exuberant that it appeared on this dimming day like a Disney diorama, presided over the scene. It was chaos, but more complicated—it was the smells of difference and the whooshing sound of our past being cast aside. We loved it.

So when the cannons boomed their notice of the revolution at 5:45 a.m., I was devastated to be facing evacuation, if we even could be evacuated. We didn't know the location of the US embassy, for heaven's sake. How naive had we been not to consider that Mexico might have a military coup?

Robert pulled on jeans and a sweater and made his way to the kitchen to find out what to do. His first clue that evacuation would not be necessary came when he noticed the cook methodically slapping her tortillas onto a hot *comal*, the steam rising and heating the cool room, her radio playing mariachi favorites—quietly, in deference to the dawn.

"*Buenos días*," she sang. Second clue.

"Um, *¿qué pasó?*" Robert stumbled on the particulars of cannons, heavy artillery, military coups, and evacuation, vocabulary words not stressed in either high school or tourist Spanish.

Fortunately, she spoke some English. "The big noises? Oh, those are *cuetes*. You'll get used to firecrackers if you're going to live in San Miguel."

Indeed, we have. It is said that *días de fiestas* claim 317 days a year in San Miguel, leaving only forty-eight lonely days without a fiesta to call their own—that there are only nine days that go without a fiesta somewhere in all of Mexico. In addition to the more common religious holidays, Mexico celebrates innumerable saints' days, feast days, a day for blessing animals, Día de los Muertos (Day of the Dead), Virgin of Guadalupe Day, Three Kings Day, and Semana Santa (Holy Week), as well as the normal array of civic anniversaries crowding the calendar. There is a Día de los Locos (Day of "the Crazies"), for which neighborhoods make floats and men dress up as well-endowed women and throw candy to the crowd. We don't even know what that is meant to celebrate.

Once there was a fiesta day for the twenty-fifth anniversary of the radio station.

Fiestas often involve not only noise but also light, a product of Mexico's longtime love affair with pyrotechnics. Fireworks makers are celebrated craftsmen. We see and hear them all, from early-morning firecrackers to great structures called *castillos* that swirl, twirl, and blaze away for our amusement while our dogs cower in the closet. Nobody does fiestas better, or has more of them, than Mexico.

The noise, the colors, the chaos and confusion drew us in as they had others before us. There are thousands of stories of how people decided to live in San Miguel, most involving people who came and never left. *Atención*, the bilingual newspaper, ran a cartoon that described our experience. In the first frame, two couples stand together, talking on the street. The residents say to the visitors, "How long will you be here?" The visitors reply, "Three weeks." As they walk away, the residents turn to each other with a wink and a smile.

"That's what they think."

Every Country Has Its Cold Remedies

I HOLD A POTTERY PLATE with a traditional *talavera* motif up to the back of a head sporting a curly black ponytail. I want to buy a matching one from this narrow wooden stall at the local market, but I cannot get *la señorita*'s attention. Her eyes are glued to the small television screen in the corner.

"*Señorita*, do you have another one like this?"

"No." She does not turn around.

I can see the matching plate just beyond her left hand, but she doesn't. She is in the grip of what may be the number-one entertainment genre in the universe, a Mexican pastime filled with jostling, brawling, and maneuvering for position. No, it is not *fútbol*—it is the telenovela, a serialized daily drama completely Latin American but wildly popular from Africa to Asia, Argentina to Afghanistan. Some estimate that two billion people are in the same grip this woman is. As a point of reference, that is 33 percent of the world's population.

On the screen, the gorgeous, aristocratic daughter of a

general, in love with a poor soldier, is being forced to marry a wealthy landowner to save her family from bankruptcy, not knowing that the poor soldier is the long-lost son of another, wealthier landowner! *¡Caray!*

If the threat of a tragic marriage were my only competition, I might be able to get the plates. But if a kidnapping, the murder of a priest, or steamy sex lurks, my interest in ceramics will pass without notice. This causes me to want to scream, *Look at me! I need these two dishes right now, and instead of helping me, you are mesmerized by a low-budget melodrama with poor production value!* But even a type A personality with impatience issues like me understands that *la señorita* doesn't care about my problems.

Personally, I prefer US soap operas. Telenovelas are too over-the-top for me. I know. I can hear people saying, "But Carol, they are *both* over-the-top." Yes, they may seem the same to the undiscerning connoisseur, but there are fine points of difference. Telenovelas have a beginning and an end, while soaps go on forever. I will admit that soap operas cannot rival the improbable plotlines, the melodramatic acting, and the bodacious breasts on the telenovelas, but I love that the soaps march into perpetuity and routinely resurrect previously dead characters. At my age, that is optimism I can believe in.

The telenovela is one of Mexico's biggest exports, with tremendous powers of persuasion at home and abroad. In a land where many more people watch television than read newspapers, telenovelas are often used to educate the public on modern views of issues such as domestic violence, homosexuality, and even male pattern baldness. And people take their telenovelas seriously. The BBC reported in 2006 that after being threatened in a grocery store by protesters who were angered by a plotline, a Venezuelan telenovela writer rewrote the final script to allow the wife of a cheating husband to get a divorce instead of reconciling with him.

There are those who will claim you can learn Spanish through telenovelas. This appeals to me. I have memorized "You are not the father of my baby!" for the next big family dinner with my ex-husband. If I am ever involved in a Stephen King version of Noah's Ark, I will be ready with "*Gracias a Dios*, he was eaten by the coyotes!" or the ever-useful "By the way, your brother was ripped to shreds by a shark."

But while I await the day these exciting events unfold, I have decided to write my own telenovela. I have not been able to develop an appetite for eating cactus, so I will try to warm up to *this* uniquely Mexican product. After all, my life often feels like a melodrama. A greater familiarity with the conventions of the telenovela genre may help me to improve my attitude toward it.

I am at a disadvantage because I have never been in a coma, had amnesia, found out the person I thought was my uncle is my father, or been switched with another baby at birth (as far as I know, at least). Nevertheless, in the true spirit of the telenovela, I am going to rise above my lack of misfortune.

I will call it *Como Tornan los Gringos: Where Honest People Suffer at the Hands of Adversity but Where Right Will Prevail, Although It Could Take a Year or More.* The main characters will be *los gringos*: La Señora, played by me, and *mi esposo*, my husband, now known as Señor Roberto, with a pharmacist and a doctor in minor roles.

Announcer: "And now we bring you today's installment of *Como Tornan los Gringos*, where we go with La Señora and Señor Roberto back to the United States to dispose of a lifetime's worth of possessions. In the prior episode, *los gringos* battled the forces of ignorance—theirs—when their Mexican house construction faced a shutdown by the city and the plumber installed the washer so that it 'walked' across an entire room like a lumbering robot while in the spin cycle. Now we join *los gringos* on a winter visit to Philadelphia, USA, to pack up their belongings and move them to Mexico."

Act One: After complicated maneuvers requiring pickups and drop-offs at the international movers' warehouse, *los gringos* congratulate themselves on how well it's going.

"*¡Viva México!* Living the dream!" they cry. High fives!

On to cleaning out the basement—a task guaranteed to lead to one of the mandatory telenovela subplots: a stay in a mental hospital.

Suddenly, La Señora grabs her throat with one hand and her forehead with the other.

"*¡Maldita sea!*" she cries, holding her *cara dramática*, her "dramatic face."

Stage Note: Saying, "¡Maldita sea!" or "Damn it!" is very popular in telenovelas, where cursing life in general is often necessary. Close-up on the cara dramática. Telenovela characters have a large repertoire of these melodramatic expressions.

La Señora has been struck with a pounding headache and a razor-sharp throat pain. A visit to the pharmacist, who recommends aspirin and throat lozenges, is accompanied by the dramatic chanting of "*¡No lo puedo creer!*"

Stage Note: "¡No lo puedo creer!" or "I can't believe it!" is the most common exclamation in telenovelas because so much happens that cannot be believed. This is an expression useful for everyday life in Mexico.

Act Two: La Señora stumbles into the dank, mildewed basement. The sore throat is gone, but chills and fever rack her body as she makes heart-wrenching decisions about what will join her in Mexico and what will be consigned to the scrap heap of Craigslist. What will she do with a cashmere scarf? Or the long double strand of pearls Señor Roberto gave her when she graduated from law school and that she wore every single day as a lawyer? Who needs cashmere and pearls in Mexico?

"*¡Maldita sea!*" she cries, looking out on a sea of boxes.

The plan to uproot their lives to Mexico and abandon a lifetime of belongings now seems like something dreamed up by a kinetic kindergarten class sipping espresso and gorging on Halloween candy. But La Señora keeps her head up, more or less like Mimi dying of consumption in *La Bohème*, emoting splendidly until the moment of death.

Stage Note: Close-up of the pharmacist's recommendations du jour: *a thermometer, Robitussin, and Advil Cold & Sinus.*

Act Three: The pearls safely packed away, La Señora adorns herself in a necklace of dread, every bead a different worry. Her temperature clocks in at 102 degrees. She has a sudden onset of cold feet not entirely caused by her frigid Philadelphia basement. Can she walk away from the life she used to live, a culture she at least thinks she understands, a language (English) that she can speak for hours (days, even, according to Señor Roberto) without faltering? Maybe she is done with the "you are what you drive" mentality, but saying good-bye to second-day delivery of an Eileen Fisher sweater made of yak yarn from herds cared for by Tibetan nomadic tribes? Is that even reasonable?

Stage Note: The camera goes tight on La Señora from the neck up—bodacious breasts are not her strong point. She contemplates how she used to be important because other people said she was, and if they are not in Mexico, which they are not, who will she be? Fade-out with today's pharmacy receipt: NyQuil, Kleenex, cough drops, and zinc tablets.

"I cannot do it." La Señora wrings her hands. "I cannot go back and live in Mexico." Tears, along with other fluids from the eyes and nose, flow together with mascara into the newly purchased Kleenex.

Señor Roberto gingerly clears his throat. He detects

disaster in this shifting psychological quicksand. He asks, "But why, why, *mi preciosa?*"

Stage Note: Señor Roberto realizes that a misstep here could lead directly to the mental-hospital subplot and an expensive psychiatric frolic unlikely to be covered by their new health insurance. This is a difficult scene: Señor Roberto's cara dramática *must show his firm belief that La Señora is overreacting, but La Señora cannot suspect that. The foundation of the telenovela is deception.*

La Señora sobs and hiccups.

"Because if they don't have throat lozenges, Robitussin, Advil, Advil Cold & Sinus, cough drops, zinc tablets, and NyQuil, I could die." She knows Mexico has Kleenex.

"My dear La Señora, star of *Como Tornan los Gringos,* of course they will. You'll see. Not the same things, but good things nonetheless. This is a difficult time, my pumpkin."

La Señora cringes. Large, orange, and round is not an appealing connotation for a woman of a certain age.

"Señora, you have lost sight of the shoreline in the foggy mists of the transition, but I see the future in my heart. Trust me, it will work out fine."

La Señora chews her thumbnail.

"Faith, Señora. You need faith. That, and a dozen more black plastic trash bags."

Stage Note: Adhering to the time-tested telenovela formula, Señor Roberto validates and promotes the right way of thinking. La Señora is a "doubter," one who is not yet ready but who will adopt the proper attitude before the end of the program. Real telenovelas have at least one "doubter" who never sees the light and is punished, perhaps by being eaten by a crocodile just so the audience doesn't miss the message. But since we have certified that no one died making my master-piece, you won't see that here.

Act Four: Resigned to living the nightmare previously known as the dream, La Señora and Señor Roberto board their flight to Mexico. Back in San Miguel and faced with La Señora's declining health, Señor Roberto calls a doctor picked at random from the telephone directory. The doctor is at the movies. She offers to come at once.

Stage Note: This last part may need to be played as a pharmaceutically-induced hallucination, because no one in the US audience will believe it possible to reach a doctor, much less persuade her to make a house call, at 9:00 p.m. on New Year's Eve.

Dr. Sylvia arrives at the sickbed and gazes at the patient.

"*¿Cómo está, señora?*"

La Señora, coughing: "*¿Bien, Doctora, y usted? ¿Cómo está su familia?*"

Stage Note: While it may not seem realistic that a person dying from a ruthless respiratory disease would ask about the doctor's family, remember, Mexicans are polite even on their deathbeds.

Dr. Sylvia: "*No lo puedo creer,* you have *la gripe! ¡Maldita sea!*"

With a powerful backhand, she sweeps the Advil,

Advil Cold & Sinus, Robitussin, zinc tablets, cough drops, and NyQuil into the wet, tissue-filled trash can. Señor Roberto's eyes widen as he follows the arc of the expensive, patented, and trademarked remedies into the abyss.

"Call *la farmacia*! You need an atomic nebulizer, sulfa drugs, and balsam-menthol skunk syrup."

La Señora smiles wanly, ruefully aware that not only has she left the soap operas of the United States behind, but she has also joined her future to the pharmaceuticals of Mexico. Colds, like life, happen everywhere. There may be no cure, but every country has its cold remedies.

Stage Note: I would be liking Javier Bardem for the role of the Mexican pharmacist, but in Mexico we never see him. La farmacia *delivers.*

SECTION TWO

THERE IS WELCOME HERE

"Let us be joyous, friends,
for there is welcome here."
—AYOCUAN, FIFTEENTH-CENTURY CHICHIMECA POET

"Let Us Be Joyous, Friends ..."

ONE FRIGID DAY, years ago, I went to the parking garage in Chicago to get my car, and it was not in my assigned space. I experienced a disorienting moment of disbelief, a sensation of falling like Alice down the rabbit hole, a moment when logic left me and my eyes, ears, and mind failed. I walked around that empty spot for twenty minutes, stomping my frozen feet and blowing into my gloved hands, knowing the car should be there, trying to convince myself the car was there, and hoping against logic that the car would reappear.

Such moments of disbelief are a regular occurrence when you live in Mexico.

One summer day, I went out into the street to find a small workshop. Armed with the street name and the number, I didn't bother to ask myself, as I usually do when I set off *a la calle*, "What could go wrong?" Because really, when you try to locate a business on a three-block road in a small town, what *could* go wrong?

Lost in the middle of this dusty lane, I called home to

Señor Roberto. I wanted to confirm the address before my internal body temperature and my anger surpassed the oppressive May heat.

"I can't find number thirty-six. Is that the right number?"

"Their business card says number thirty-six. Do you see number thirty-four or thirty-eight?"

"No, the street ends at thirty-two."

"Are you sure?" His voice held just a hint of condescension.

I wanted to scream, "Am I sure? Of course I'm sure, because I learned number sequencing in the second grade!" But instead I pretended the phone had died, and I sat on the curb to think.

The day's heat had driven everyone inside, so I rested alone on the cool gray stone to review my options and corral my temper. "Ave María," which plays daily on Radio San Miguel at noon, filtered out from a closed door behind me. I saw a young man approaching on the narrow sidewalk, his backpack and uniform of sweater and plaid pants identifying him as a student. He angled into the street to avoid stepping on me.

I jumped up to block his path, in case he tried to ignore me, and said, "*Disculpe, dónde está número treinta y seis?*"

"I don't know, *señora*, but who do you look for?"

"The *tienda* that makes silver frames." What I actually said was closer to "the store that makes dish structures." My Spanish evaporates in heat.

"*Por supuesto, señora*, I know them. I will walk you."

And back we went. Sure enough, there it was, number thirty-six, nestled without any distinguishing numbers or name on the facade, in between number twenty-five and number twenty-seven.

On days like this, right after being fascinated with all of the new cultural experiences, then angry at the fact that Mexico is not the United States, I have to find my way to acceptance. Here is what I am learning to do:

1. Love imperfection. I am learning to love it like I love my ill-behaved dogs that bring me great joy despite their undisciplined habit of using expensive shoes as chew toys. Loving imperfection is difficult for me. I am well indoctrinated into the religion of perfection topped off with a strong belief in my ability to control the universe.

2. Appreciate that the history of every nation marks not just the past but also the present. In the United States, we have a long history of freedom. Mexicans have a very different story. Coming here to live, I dove headfirst into a cultural river; learning something about the history of Mexico is a worthwhile swimming lesson. When people tell me they want to come here because of the low cost of living, I recommend considering Arkansas. When people tell me they want to come here because they imagine how wonderful it must be to have inexpensive household help, I smile and suggest they might want to learn to love dust. Do

not come for the less expensive lifestyle—or one that includes the domestic help you cannot buy in the United States. Come here to love Mexico, or be willing to try.

3. Accept that Mexican culture offers an opportunity to be clueless every day. It can be frightening to lose control of the world or liberating to let go of old assumptions. I try for the latter. Understanding Mexican culture is like being an archeologist —it requires digging and sifting through layers of language, history, geography, religion, art, and politics. The job is never done, but the reward is seeing Mexican people, even for just a second, for who they are: people who value family, respect, trust, and time to enjoy whatever they have.

4. Conquer Spanish. Honestly, I know I never will, but it doesn't matter. It's all about trying. Brain science tells us we need to constantly exercise our aging brains; new language skills are one way to do that. Here is the bonus: being able to talk to Mexicans, even in halting, blocky Spanglish, is such a treat—well, for them maybe less a treat and more a comic interlude. Mexicans are extremely encouraging of our attempts to communicate, even when it includes a high ratio of sign language, sound effects, arm waving, and a vocabulary of words performed with a tone-deaf Spanish accent.

5. Need less. That day in Chicago when my car disappeared, I discovered it had been towed. I had mistakenly parked it in another owner's space, and I didn't know it had been resting in the Chicago impound lot for over five weeks. It had never occurred to me that I didn't need a car. But I didn't. Here in Mexico, I am pushed by the scarcity of dill pickles, aged cheese, and low-fat, sugar-free yogurt to step outside my sense of who I am, safe in the knowledge that I will survive nicely without so many things I once firmly believed I needed.

6. Believe in the validity of all cultures. I am a patriot as well as an expatriate. I cry when I hear "God Bless America" and almost all country-and-western songs. The United States is a remarkable place where many people, myself included, have been given tremendous opportunities to make something better of their lives. In Mexico, I look at the best and worst of my culture with new eyes. I see we are good people, brave people, smart people. But I also see we are not the only people and our way is not the only way. This is a foreign concept in the United States today.

7. Travel to other parts of Mexico. When I do, I experience the richness of regional differences but feel the same culture of warmth and civility everywhere. Señor Roberto once asked a stranger

sitting behind us on a full-to-bursting bus in Mexico City if she knew how to get to Casa Azul in Coyoacán. She did not. Three minutes later, she tapped him on the shoulder. "These people"— she pointed to a woman and two teenage daughters, jammed farther back in the aisle—"they are going there, and they will take you." She had found a family who would guide us all the way to our destination, out of the way of theirs. That is the heart of Mexico, the cultural motif that connects small towns and big cities, even Mexico City, the second-largest city in the world.

I see the faults—of course I do. Even blissful relationships have bad days. Experts tell us happy marriages are those in which the positive interactions outweigh the negative by a ratio of five to one.

And so it is here. Street numbers that follow no discernible pattern: score one; making a new friend who walks me to my destination: score five.

LEARNING TO LOVE IMPERFECTION

ONCE, IN A TWO-HOUR Internet training session I conducted for lawyers, the telephone connection failed, causing a twenty-second delay. When the class ended, a participant asked, "Will you be getting back to me to let me know what happened?"

I hesitated because the interruption had been so minor I couldn't remember what happened. "No," I said, guessing he referred to the brief break. "I don't think so."

"Why not?"

"Because I don't know what happened. It was a momentary technological glitch. The world, after all, is not a perfect place," I joked.

"Well," he said in a peevish voice, "it should be."

I know how he feels. I am well indoctrinated into the cult of perfection. I used to hang my clothes on color-coded plastic hangers. Have I mentioned that all my file folders have white labels with black letters that march uniformly out of a machine? That I consider a labeling machine necessary for good mental health?

This approach does have its place (brain surgery and space missions come to mind), but an unwarranted focus on perfection can lead to chronic disappointment. When we use "perfect" as our standard, our real but highly flawed world inhabited by spectacularly imperfect human beings becomes inferior and can never measure up.

In the United States, we waste so much energy trying to control our environment, stamping out imperfection and making the universe "perfect" according to our own cultural vision. For example, US homeowners' associations for condominiums and gated communities control the housing of 57 million people. It often appears that their major responsibility is to protect their inhabitants from children playing on sidewalks or the well-known danger of different-colored mailboxes.

Mexicans, on the other hand, are not as interested in the pursuit of perfection and control as we are. They accept the world as imperfect and do not ask it to change. Instead, they allow and embrace everything. Houses are painted in outrageous shades: a mustard-yellow door argues amiably with walls of a pink hue most closely associated with a flamingo lawn ornament, all neighboring a mottled, peeling turquoise wall.

The Mexican philosophy on imperfection is captured by the expression *ni modo*, loosely translated as, "Well, what can you do?" accompanied by a shrug. Another useful phrase in describing life's imperfections is *no pasa nada*, which means "nothing happened" or "no worries."

But I do worry. I worry that my housekeeper,

Magali, mops twenty times more frequently than she dusts.

"Why? Why mop again?" I cry.

"Because every day when I broom the carpet, it makes the floor dirty."

What the hell? *Broom* the carpet? "Why not use the vacuum cleaner?" I am referring to the high-tech machine that I practically carried to San Miguel on my back.

"I will, *señora*. Tomorrow."

I know she won't, because she doesn't like it. She likes the broom. Then I remember *ni modo*.

"*Ni modo*," I say, picking up the dust cloth with a shrug. Why worry just because I can eat off the floors but not the table? In another year or two I will be sanguine enough to say, "*No pasa nada*."

Our experience with construction is another example of the impracticability of clinging to perfection. For example, after five days in San Miguel, we decided to buy the perfect house. In the interest of full disclosure, it was not a house; it was a housing complex, a drab lineup of five 1950s-era apartments marching up a hill, bordering a common passageway. It looked like the love child of Disrepair and Disinterest.

We did not consider that we were in a foreign country where we did not exactly speak the language. We saw the promise of perfection, a space with such light and possibility that we could not walk away. The location whispered "perfect," too: a block from the Jardín, the mariachi-laden, people-watching mecca and historic center of San Miguel, on a cobblestone lane a friend once called "the best street in the world."

We were naive. We did not see that it might be complicated. We did not see that we were in a land that loves mole—a sauce requiring the roasting, toasting, pureeing, reconstituting, frying, and heaven only knows what other processing of twenty-eight different ingredients in a *molcajete*, a lava-rock bowl. (Note: do not try the roasting and toasting of chile peppers at home, or you may find, as I did, that smoking chiles can clear a room faster than tear gas.) No, we did not see that—not in the beginning. In a perfect world, that world we believed we controlled, construction would be a joy.

Señor Roberto and I were confident in our experience with construction. He focused on demolition with an emphasis on fighting for space, because, like the old woman who lived in a shoe, we never had enough. I was the director of ambience. I came in with the furniture, the artwork, and the decorative elements. We adhered to what our favorite designer once told us: "First the bones, then the muscle, and then the skin." I provided the skin.

And what skin it was! Mexican colors, seductive in those burnished sun shades, rubbed into concrete, those different flavors and hues of ceramics, textiles—they beckoned me with enthusiasm. So off across Mexico I went.

I visited a *tienda* in Tlaquepaque, a craft town near Guadalajara, and saw a ceramic sculpture so whimsical, so joyful, so primary in its colors, I laughed out loud.

I asked the shopkeeper, "*¿Quién hace este?*"

"Señor Ortega makes this, *señora. Él vive en Las Huertas.*"

"Can I go there? What is the address?"

"No address, *señora.* It's close by. Just ask for him in the village." She fluttered her hand off in the direction of Baja California. I questioned how I would find him with this imprecise approach, but she appeared so matter-of-fact, I thought, *Well, why not?*

I found Las Huertas and I asked for Señor Ortega in the village. A stranger took me to his house, and Señor Ortega invited me in. His kiln, fired by scrap wood, sat in his backyard, propped up on concrete and old wooden pallets. His brothers and nephews painted clay animals at a long, sloping table on a dirt floor in a nearby shed with a corrugated metal roof. Improbably enough, there was a mission statement and an organizational chart on the bare concrete wall. For 300 pesos (approximately US$24), I bought a big, red ceramic bus, imperfect in its shape and faulty in its proportions but filled to overflowing with little clay passengers and a man flying with wild abandon on the roof.

Perfection did not find us at Cinco Flores, our Mexican home renovation project. To our surprise, when the contractor finished remodeling several apartments, he announced we owed him an amazing sum of money. He knew this, he said, because he kept a shoe box with our payments and receipts in it and the box was filled with unpaid bills and no pesos to pay them.

There is a casual approach to money here that frequently works to my benefit. If I am at a small *tienda*, buying *limones* or soap or tortillas without exact change, my bill is often rounded down to the amount I am carrying. I get my purchase with a request to return someday with the difference.

But the sheer volume of the money involved in the renovation project seemed to warrant a more rigorous bookkeeping system. Fortunately, we'd gotten the contractor's signature for all the payments he'd received. When he left, so did our confidence in managing Mexican construction.

Soon, the city inspector came and threatened to put a dreaded OBRA SUSPENDIDA (WORK SUSPENDED) notice on our building, signaling the same level of shame and deviation from communal mores as a scarlet letter. The same contractor had neglected to obtain an essential permit. Then he turned us in for failing to have it after the shoe box incident. While Señor Roberto negotiated with the inspector, I cowered in the corner of my office, visions of Mexican prison from old Zorro movies tap-dancing in my stomach, churning the *huevos revueltos* I'd scrambled for breakfast. Señor Roberto dodged the shutdown by gamely holding forth on the situation's injustice and then hiring the same city inspector to help us get the missing permit.

Construction continued. Countertops were built too narrow to accommodate a stove, causing the heat to build and threaten an explosion sufficient to annihilate the cook. Furniture measured and remeasured was returned an inexplicable four inches too short. Our plumber, a happy character who careened through the cobblestone streets in a tiny Volkswagen filled to overflowing with young assistant plumbers, hooked up hot water to the toilet, allowing me to dream, if only for a minute, that Señor Roberto had installed a heated toilet seat. All this happened and more.

But not everything was a problem. In fact, some things were perfectly easy.

Because houses here do not have central heating or air-conditioning, concrete workers—*albañiles*—gouged out tracks for pipes, moving bathrooms and kitchens at will. When there wasn't enough height to accommodate a stairway, they dug the floor out twelve inches lower. To our surprise, every window, every door, stood plumb, the measurements accurate, accomplished with rudimentary tools—without even a level.

The *albañiles* were cheerful, and their smiles, laughter, and music went into every batch of the hand-mixed concrete walls that would encircle us in the days to come. They invited us to fiestas at their houses where the head of the pig killed for dinner sat like a guest on the table. At our electrician's daughter's *quinceañera*, the elaborate fifteenth-birthday party for young women, I learned why it is not a good idea to drink tequila straight, a lesson I will remember—as will Señor Roberto—for the rest of my life. During construction, I learned that Mexicans are a happy and satisfied people, perhaps because they accept the world as it is instead of striving for a perfection that can never be achieved. Could I learn to tilt in this direction?

One day during construction, an *albañil* showed me he was ready to install the clay floor tiles in the living room. As we stood together, he pointed out a stack of tiles he had put aside to be used closest to the walls, where they would not be seen.

"*¿Por qué?*" I asked.

"Because they are damaged. When they dry out in the countryside, animals walk on some and leave their prints."

I looked over at the red bus waiting to be unwrapped, remembering the expression of the clay man flying on the roof. Was he saying, "I should not be on top of this bus—too windy"? Or "*¡Qué bueno!* The view and the air up here are *magnífico*"?

Turning to the *albañil*, I said, "Put them here," pointing out a prominent place in the entry. The plumbing may be flawed and the stove may explode, but walking on the indelible imprint of small feet that once crossed these tiles is a permanent reminder that imperfection can be perfect.

Where La Patrona Gets a Cook and Gives Up Her Fantasy of Domestic Bliss

---

"SEÑORA?" LUIS FERNANDO, our cook of one week, called. "Breakfast is ready."

The patio table was resting under a huge ficus tree and set for two, a flock of birds of paradise preening in a vase in the center. The mosaic tabletop held hand-painted ceramic plates with colorful blue and green fish parading around the border. Was this a movie scene from someone else's life? I blinked as the penetrating aroma of raw garlic caused my eyes to water. Wait a minute! This wasn't French toast. It looked like . . . toast with butter and chunks of raw garlic? *What the hell?*

"So, um, what do we have for breakfast today, Luis Fernando?" I stepped carefully here. I had never had a cook.

He tilted his head, surprised I didn't recognize it.

"French toast, *señora*. It is what you asked for."

Yes, well, if a cross-cultural domestic train wreck is involved, then it is a movie of my life after all.

When we moved to Mexico, where household help is inexpensive and common, my fantasy was to have sufficient help to make our home run with Swiss efficiency—a place where mattresses would be rotated on schedule; a lively dusting and vacuuming regime would be performed every day; bathrooms would be furnished with fresh white towels; and laundry would be washed, folded, and ironed on a regular basis.

In other words, everything I never did. Ever.

In my imagination, my role would be limited and advisory. Like the Duchess of Windsor, I would set the routine, give occasional directions, and lend a gentle, guiding hand. I would then retire to my office and reemerge later to admire a calm, clean, and orderly domestic landscape.

It was a lot to want. As it turned out, it was the wrong thing to want.

Even before my fantasy met reality, I worried. I didn't want to become too pampered, like the fifteenth-century Spaniards who relied on the Jews and the Moors to do their dirty work and then couldn't change a lightbulb for 400 years after they shortsightedly expelled them. Hailing from an allegedly egalitarian and socially mobile democracy, I did not want to become an oppressor. I wanted to run my home less like the women in *The Help* and more like those portrayed, however unrealistically, on *Downton Abbey*.

In reality, I had no experience with household help. As a lawyer with a grueling schedule, I had a scant four hours of housecleaning help every two weeks. Now, working part-time consulting on legal issues, I had Josefina the housekeeper and Juan the gardener every day but Sunday. Their services were included with *la casa* that we rented for a year while we renovated our house. Totally by accident and through various cultural complications, I also got a *cocinero*, a cook.

My fantasy of the well-run, blissful household had not even extended to the kitchen, so I was surprised when I became the employer of a *cocinero*. It all started with a conversation with Señora Rosalba, the agent who rented us the house. I wanted to meet with her to see if the housekeeper might actually, well, keep house.

"Señora Rosalba, I don't want to complain." I cast my eyes down in a humble attempt to blunt the fact that although I did not want to complain, I was going to do so. "The housekeeper, Josefina, has a baby that she brings to work. She can't get any housework done, and she doesn't cook."

"*Bebé*! What *bebé*? Isn't she cleaning for you?"

I hated to raise the issue of the baby, because, really, he was delightful—a roly-poly, dark-haired boy whose favorite activity was to suck on his toe.

"No, she is not cleaning, and when she is cleaning, I am watching the baby."

"This is outrageous! You should not be babysitting this baby! You must have a cook." This non sequitur would require a difficult leap in English; in Spanish, remember, I was dancing backward in high heels.

"A cook? *¿Un cocinero?* But, *señora*, I don't think we need *un cocinero*."

This represents the simplified English translation. These demurrals must be said with the deferential, nonconfrontational Spanish formality that marks the language of respect. I call it "sing-songy" talk.

Translated, it went, "My dear, esteemed Señora Rosalba, while I trust implicitly in your very practical suggestions and have the highest regard for your deep understanding, I wonder if perhaps this step is necessary. I fear it might cause you too much trouble." I signaled telepathically through long eye contact that if Josefina just did a hint of cleaning and a dash of cooking, all would be well.

Señora Rosalba drew herself up to her full four feet, ten inches, which included the highest heels ever seen in North America except for New York City (which, it must be said, does not have many cobblestone streets).

"*Señora*, if you can afford a cook, you must employ one. Mexicans need work." Señora Rosalba's tone of finality signaled the discussion's end. So much for cross-cultural telepathy. I was not prepared for this argument, so I thought, *What the hell—maybe I do need a cook.* (Note: Until I moved to Mexico, I never once said, "What the hell." I have tried to make *¡Caray, caray!* my exclamation of choice, but it is not as expressive as "what the hell," and I don't know what it means. *Ni modo.* Mexicans love swearing, and off-color and colorful expressions, so I will find something in Spanish eventually.)

Luis Fernando was a friend of Señora Rosalba with experience as a *cocinero*. He came and met us. He had a wonderful sparkle in his eyes that we knew would breathe laughter into our days, and he could shop and cook. In Mexico, just grocery shopping, while charming, chews up time for a person with work obligations. Every little *tienda* has its specialty: meat in one, chicken in another, fruits and vegetables in an altogether different location. Having someone to do that and cook, too? It sounded like a good idea. No, it sounded like a *great* idea. My domestic-bliss dreams took an uptick.

My fantasy did not take into account that the work culture in Mexico today is a long thread connecting the present to a colonial past. More than two hundred years after independence, more than one hundred years after the revolution, times have changed, but not completely.

In colonial Mexico, the foundation of social and economic status was caste, or *casta*. The Spaniards diced caste into numerous racial categories: *peninsulares*, those purebred Spaniards born in Spain, a higher caste than those Spaniards born in Mexico (known as *criollos*), the progeny of Spaniards and indigenous people (*mestizos*), or the children of Spaniards and Negroes (*mulatos*). By 1821, when castes were abolished, Mexico had more than one hundred of them: *castizos, cambujos, calpamulatos, zambos* —a veritable declension of oppression. When a baby was born, a priest assigned a caste based on the perceived ratio of Spanish-to-indigenous or Negro blood. People remained in this designated caste for their lifetime—with no incentive for merit, no working harder for a better life.

The lower castes were bound to the haciendas, the huge land grants given to the *conquistadores* and the Catholic Church by the Spanish crown. These vast entitlements operated as semi-feudal systems, where the *patrón* was responsible for the hacienda workers and the workers were dependent on the *patrón*. Survival tactics for life in this often-ruthless place, where you could not speak without permission, were: don't bring bad news to the boss, avoid conflict, don't initiate anything.

Traces of caste and *patrón*, rusted by centuries of tears, have creaked into twenty-first-century Mexico long past their legal abolition. This is not surprising, since the grandparents of many of today's domestic workers were born on the hacienda's desecrated land. The tyranny of subjugation put most Mexicans on the bottom rungs of the social and economic ladder. The unholy alliance of poverty, poor education, religion, and the insularity of large families has kept countless people on those same rungs—bound now by class, not caste.

It is understandable, then, that domestic workers here do not have the same approach to work that we take for granted in the United States. They work hard, but they work differently. The lessons from the *hacienda* run deep. If the hot-water heater stops working, the housekeeper will wash the dishes in cold water for days until I return and stand in a shower that never turns warm. No one wants to give La Patrona bad news. Mexican workers are also loath to criticize or supervise other Mexican workers.

Criticism is seen as destructive to community harmony.

If plants are in the final stages of *plaga*, the gardener will not take the initiative to ask for an insect spray. No, he will wait until they die or I notice, whichever comes first. And if I do spot the sad, limp leaves with alarm and question him about what we should do, he is reluctant to tell me. It might be the wrong answer. He will look to me, a foreigner with a black thumb, to tell him. It does not matter what the garden needs—it matters what I, La Patrona, want, even if it is wrong. And if La Patrona asks for French toast, do not under any circumstances mention that you don't know how to make it.

Mexico is a paternalistic world where the winds of caste and *hacienda* life still whisper, where the *patrón* may pay low wages but also shoulder significant responsibilities, both legal and cultural, for workers. The same word in English is "patron," one who protects or supports. Because of Mexico's history, domestic work here is not a simple matter of exchanging labor for money.

As *patrones*, we consult with lawyers about children permanently expelled from school and with doctors about cousins with rare illnesses; contribute to the installation of water pipes and the administration of medicines; and buy so many third-birthday, confirmation, first-communion, and *quinceañera* cakes that we have the bakery on speed dial. We beg our friends north of the border for so much money, for so many old computers, clothes, school supplies, and ibuprofen for arthritic knees that I imagine the arrival of our e-mails is as welcome as the note from the kindergarten teacher announcing your child has lice. We are *patrones*; this is what we do.

After the French Toast Caper, Luis Fernando became a part of our life, moving with us from the rented house, where we ate the toast with butter and scraped off the garlic, to our own house when renovations were completed. His sense of humor delighted us daily. We helped him and his sister and nephews buy a house, an unheard-of accomplishment for many working-class Mexicans. We lived through his struggle with alcohol addiction and the months of his rehabilitation, hoping for the best, paying his salary, and cooking for ourselves.

So it was that when we fired him for stealing, my disillusioned tears fell like candy from a piñata. I wept not only for lost mole but also for lost faith. He knew it was wrong, he said, but he had been robbed and he needed the money, so he passed the injustice on to us, *los patrones*, who were more able to absorb it than he.

Our Mexican friends tell us that we gringos make a mistake when we try to help our workers beyond what the law requires, when we try to boost them up and over poverty's edge; when we cross a line that Mexicans see and we don't. I appreciate that view. In navigating these complexities, it is difficult to distinguish between wise compassion and idiot compassion, where good intentions merge with guilt, maybe a desire to see ourselves as kind, perhaps an inability to say no.

But I have upward mobility in my cultural DNA. I want people to do better. So many have reached down to give me their hand along my journey; should not that debt be repaid now? It is hard to know when to accede to Mexican culture and when to declare firmly, as I have on occasion, "I know this is Mexico, but I am a gringa and I need to do it another way."

In the meantime, we still had a baby and a dusty house. Señora Rosalba assured me that she would speak to Josefina about not bringing the baby to work, and soon he disappeared. *Solved*, I thought naively, not knowing that solutions do not come that easily in Mexico. After a few days, I happened to walk past the "maid's quarters," where I saw . . . wait—another child! I discovered that Josefina's nine-year-old daughter now came to work with her mother to watch the baby. What the hell?

We called Señora Rosalba. We spoke firmly. We spoke righteously. We would not allow a nine-year-old to be removed from school to babysit.

I began to argue with myself.

No. A nine-year-old belongs in school.

But Josefina travels in from the campo *far outside town; no child care for her.*

No. No baby.

But Josefina works to feed her daughter, her son, and the baby. What will become of them?

No. It is Josefina's problem, not mine.

Easy for you to say. But what is she going to do?

In the end the real question was, what were *we* going to do? We wrestle with the immutable forces of culture and poverty daily as we try to land on the side of wise compassion. None of it is easy. Sometimes I despair over the hot water turned cold, plants now dead, and other offenses large and small. But the resilience, laughter, and loyalty of the Mexicans who surround me make it a fair trade. Given that we hope to be here until death do us part, we ask ourselves, how do we want to treat the people who are likely to be delivering us to the doorway of heaven?

It had been many years since I had enjoyed the companionship of a baby. So when he joined me in my office every day, my fantasies faded but the rich ambiguities of domestic bliss increased. I knew it was not the way the hacienda *patrona* would have done it, but I am a gringa, and I needed to do it my way.

SAVING MY BREATH

AS A RUNNER, I think a lot about breath. Even if your lungs are strong enough to sing "The Ride of the Valkyries" fortissimo, you could be short of breath in San Miguel de Allende. First, the altitude is 6,500 feet. Second, we have steep hills. Third, we have people, bicycles, donkeys, and cars all sharing narrow sidewalks, cobblestone streets, and dirt paths. So much breath has to go into just staying upright.

When I began running here, I noticed that the strangers I passed spoke to me.

"*Buenos días, señora,*" they called out.

And I, panting like a dog, thought, *Are you kidding me? You are delusional if you imagine that I can talk and run at the same time! Why are you speaking to me? Do I even know you?*

I went to a class at our local Spanish school, where the master teacher, Warren Hardy, gave us a useful lesson on Mexican culture. I learned that Mexicans love formality, courtesy, and ceremony. In the United States, I would not say hello to every stranger I encounter as I walk down the street, nor would they speak to me. But, here in Mexico, particularly in small towns, they have what I call the Dance of the *Buenos Días*. The dance is part of a complex of rules, a formalized code of courtesy, *cortesía*, begun long ago and still taught today. It dictates what the polite person will do in certain circumstances, including how to greet another traveler on the street. Participating in these rituals guarantees not only a greater understanding of the gentle ways of this country but also that you will need to save more breath than you imagined.

Ready to master the four-position *buenos días* dance?

First position: If the person coming toward you is on the same side of the street as you are, one of you is going to have to step off the narrow sidewalk. Be ready for the footwork and balance this requires. You should be that person, unless the other party is much younger.

Second position: As in ballet, the second position is an opening. Make eye contact and smile as you pass. Remember, this could be someone walking, running, bicycling, or leading a donkey. Don't worry about people in cars. They have their own problems.

Third position: Nod your head deeply. Feel the respect of this gesture and its alignment with the idea that the world is an open and magical place where we actually do wish strangers well.

Fourth position: Sing out, "*Buenos días, señor,*" the translation of which is said to be "May God give you good days." Note that these words are not muttered or whispered. No, they are delivered forcefully, with feeling. The stranger will make eye contact (if he hasn't already), smile, nod his head, and respond with "*Buenos días*" or "*Buen día, señora.*"

Keep in mind there are two variables here: time of day and the title of the person to whom you are speaking. First, master the time of day. *Buenos días* has a precise shelf life—it ends at noon. If you are out on the street and you do not have a watch, you will know it is noon by listening to the church bells, which tell the time in fifteen-minute increments, or by listening to Radio San Miguel, which is on in every shop and home in San Miguel and plays "Ave María" every day at noon. When you hear "Ave María," it is time to switch to *buenas tardes*, or "good afternoon."

The ending time of *buenas tardes* is less certain and much debated. It would give us a better sense of certainty if Radio San Miguel played the Lord's Prayer when it was time to move to *buenas noches*, but instead it plays that every day at 3:00 p.m., which is too early to change from afternoon to evening. We use the sundown rule. You have to give this your best guess, but when the afternoon has dimmed to the color of *café con leche*, move to *buenas noches*.

Now on to the second variable: titles. Men are *señor*; unmarried women, or those whose status you don't know, are *señorita*; and known, married women are *señora*. Older people are *don* and *doña*. Titles are important here. I am never known as Carol. I am known in the third person as La Señora, as in, "La Señora does not want fish tacos for dinner." I mention fish tacos as that is probably what Señor Roberto wants to eat and what the cook does not want to make.

Needless to say, amid all of this, I have to keep my wits about me when I am out on the street. When I run early in the morning, I come upon what feels like an endless flow of people going to work on the cobblestone streets and the dirt paths outside town.

"*Buenos días, señor.*"

"*Buenos días, señora.*"

I love this simple ritual and its gentle benediction. I firmly believe that someday brain scientists will discover that wishing strangers well on a daily basis creates some kind of useful chemical that soothes the frazzled soul. (Stay tuned on this theory.) Whether it is a young man with purple-tinted hair and earphones in his ears or an ancient woman with a mahogany face like a dried-up apple who is carrying tortillas in a bucket to sell door-to-door, everyone knows the rules. These greetings carry a tender respect, blind to the usual issues of class, race, and economics. Where *buenos días* is concerned, we are all wading in this river of life together.

But to flow with that river while running, I must save enough breath. In doing so, I have come to feel that this is a good practice. So when I am frustrated because, despite constant urging, the electric company cannot figure out how to send a bill for two years but can send someone to turn off the electricity for nonpayment, I make an effort to save my breath. When it takes seven trips to the agency that collects taxes so that we can beg to pay ours, I try to save my breath. It's not that I ignore everything, although many things are worth ignoring. But it just may be worthwhile to wait for the right opportunity and to say less.

This works not just in Mexico. The United States would be a better and more civilized place if, before entering into public discourse, our more voluble politicians and television commentators were forced to run smiling and nodding up a steep hill at an altitude of 6,500 feet while looking into the eyes of their fellow man and calling out, "*Buenos días, señor.*" Less might be said, but what would be said might be more worthwhile.

WHERE THE DOCTOR LOOKS LIKE ANTONIO BANDERAS AND COMES TO YOUR HOUSE WHEN YOU ARE SICK

YOU WOULD BE AMAZED at how sitting on a bench in the Jardín, the quintessential Mexican town square, can create a warm sense of well-being, *bienestar*—a permission to be alive and to live life on a human scale. Vendors push their food carts into place, soon to produce *hamburguesas* or cut-up fruit for sale, young lovers lounge on the perimeter walls intertwined like pretzels, backpack-clad children in plaid school uniforms, hair braided or slicked straight up, all stream by, engaged in the movement of daily life.

On this day, I was enjoying the smell of spring in the midmorning sun when a woman of about my vintage deposited herself next to me to rest her weary tourist feet. She asked the number-one question *estadounidenses* (North Americans from the United States) of a certain age want to know when they learn I live in Mexico.

"But what about health care?"

Just like that, I went from all contented to ill tempered. That is the problem with *bienestar*; it is as perishable as a ripe banana.

It was the subtext to this question that made me cranky: the belief that US health care is tied up in a gold-embossed box with a sparkly bow, while Mexico's is in a brown paper bag. That bright package may be expensive, but it is not as good as you might think.

I huffed to myself, *Well, but what* about *health care?* What I said aloud was, "Well, but what about health care?" in a nice, polite voice. Really, the woman was just asking a question. How could she know that I suffer from San Miguel syndrome—an occasional, ungenerous state of impatience bordering on intolerance, experienced when my countrymen are naive, as I was before I came here?

"Do you go back to the United States when you are sick?"

My eyebrows shot up to my hairline. I tried to channel the Dalai Lama, who, I feel certain, is rarely churlish.

I explained that since we are ten hours from Texas, returning to the United States for heartburn (or an episode of San Miguel syndrome, such as I was having at that moment) is not a sustainable strategy. While I do receive health care in the United States, I also benefit from Mexican health care—a different, and often preferable, experience.

What's the problem with US health care delivery?

How about this? It's a bad bargain. The White House Office of Management and Budget reports that 30 percent of our national expenditures (in 2012, a chin-dropping $2.8 trillion) do not result in better health. We have fancy medical offices, hard-to-get appointments, cutting-edge medical tests, and mechanical and technical interventions that raise costs but do not deliver higher-quality care. We are focused on the shiny, high-priced things, when we often lack the fundamentals—including easy access to and adequate time with our doctors and a more hands-on practice of medicine.

That is what we have in Mexico. Here, health care delivery is accessible, personal, and hands-on, at least as long as you have cash. Need an ophthalmologist at 9:30 p.m. on a Thursday night (or New Year's Eve, for that matter) because your Internet research has diagnosed a detached retina? No problem. Find her in the local phone book, and call her at her house (or the movies). Meet her at her office, confirm the diagnosis, and arrange for next-day surgery at a nearby hospital. Don't have a car? The doctor will drive. Bring cash, because they don't take checks, insurance, American Express, or any other credit card—but the operation will cost 70 percent less than it would in the United States.

What if you have the digestive defection known as *el turista* at 4:30 a.m.? If even the prospect of collecting the lottery could not persuade you to get off the bathroom floor and go to the hospital, a doctor who looks like Antonio Banderas will come to your house, give you a miraculous injection, and charge US$50. If you are envious of the Antonio Banderas part, remember that when the contents of your food-processing tract have left your body many times over, in many directions, you do not look your best. You would not care if the doctor looked like Boris Karloff if he had that shot.

In San Francisco, I had the same *turista*. Since Antonio Banderas would not come to my hotel room, I struggled to the hospital emergency room. I begged for the same miraculous shot; what I received was five hours on a metal table, expensive tests, no test results, and the miraculous medicine delivered intravenously for US$1,800.

In addition to being accessible, Mexican health care delivery, like most things Mexican, is very personal. Want to ask the doctor a question? Call her on her cell phone. She will answer and talk to you. Remember, though, turnabout is fair play. When you have an appointment, the doctor may interrupt your list of symptoms to chat with another patient. Since an insurance company does not monitor your visit, you are not worried—if you need an hour, you'll get one. Mexico's medical care is the antithesis of US "health care in a hurry," where fifteen-minute appointments are the norm.

You may assume, as some people do, that Mexican medicine is slow and primitive, as though we are waiting for a donkey to deliver the equipment. In fact, medical care here can be delivered as fast as a New York pizza. Want an appointment to see your doctor? Come today. Need a stress test tomorrow—Saturday? No problem.

Your doctor has a cardiologist friend who will come in early and do the test. His office linoleum will be well worn, like his furniture, but paying him will not involve a mortgage and his diagnosis will be accurate.

What if the test shows your arteries may be clogged and you need an angiogram to see whether there is a blockage? Let's see, today is Saturday. How about Monday? Would Monday be good for you? Go to the hospital, which looks like a Hyatt hotel with medical staff, an operating room, and shiny, high-tech equipment. Not every hospital in Mexico is so advanced, but many are, especially in urban centers.

Not only are many hospitals here modern, but also many doctors are world-class. A friend, diagnosed with pancreatic cancer while he was in San Miguel, was told that his two best choices for treatment were Boston and Mexico City. When he met his oncologist, the head of the pancreatic cancer center at a premier Boston hospital, the doctor told him, "If you had gone to Mexico City, you would have been under the care of my teacher."

In part, Mexican medical care is marked by what it doesn't have rather than by what it does. There is almost nonexistent regulation. Few medicines require a prescription, and no scripts are needed for medical tests. Want to get the bad news about your cholesterol level? Go to the lab and, for a few pesos, get a report as often as you want. Feeling tired? Believe that a nice shot of vitamin B_{12} might do the trick? Toddle over to one of the local pharmacies, duck behind the counter where a dog is lounging, and drop your drawers. Just like that. I know what you're thinking—it's scary to me, too—but after a while it seems normal. I am positive that none of this, especially the dog, is legal in the United States.

Medical records are also not regulated by a chokehold of paternalism in Mexico. By contrast, I once went to my local US hospital to retrieve my mammogram films so I would have them with me in Mexico.

Without glancing up from her computer, the clerk inquired, "Where will you be taking these?"

I stopped to consider what she meant. "To my house?" I offered. I had a hunch that was the wrong answer.

"No." She gave me a disdainful glance. "What facility are you transferring these to?"

"I don't know." I don't like to discuss living in Mexico. Too many people think I am either working for the drug cartels or a product of the Witness Protection Program.

"I am sorry," she continued—but she was not, I could tell by her pinched expression—"I cannot release these to you without the name and address of the new facility."

Finally, I gave her the name of my doctor's office and skulked away like a person with criminal-behavior issues. If I were given to insomnia, I would be lying awake at night, wondering what kind of threat I pose to my own medical records.

You may be thinking, *Well, but all of this gives us*

better care. But no. According to 2010 World Health Organization statistics, Mexico expended US$962 per capita on public and private health care, and its inhabitants have a life expectancy of 77.2 years, just two and a half years lower than that of the United States, where we spend almost ten times more, $8,233. The life expectancy of thirty-four other countries, all of which spend less, is better than that of the United States. Perhaps the Affordable Care Act will improve our efficiency, but for now, *¿quién sabe?*

Last year, I developed a hard lump under the pad of my big toe. I was in the United States when it began to hurt, so I went to see a doctor. I told him I thought I had gotten a splinter while walking barefoot on the beach. After panoramic X-rays, an MRI, and two office visits, I still had no diagnosis. (Señor Roberto mentally tracks these events. "Remember when," he occasionally reminisces, "you had the twenty-five-thousand-dollar undiagnosable heart episode in Chicago?")

"Surgery," said the doctor. "Go to the hospital for pre-admittance tests. The surgery will take less than a day. You will have stitches, and you will have to stay off your foot for a while." It could all be arranged in three weeks.

I didn't have time for that. I came back to Mexico, and when it flared up again, I was in a village that had only the most rudimentary medical services—a doctor, fresh out of medical school, who was stationed there for a year, doing his national service, seeing patients, and living in a rustic building maintained by members of the community. I walked into the clinic while he was eating his lunch. I was the only patient.

"Looks like a splinter to me."

That was what I thought, too.

"Soak it in hot salt water and see if you can coax it to come out."

A day later, Señor Roberto persuaded a quarter-inch splinter to exit, and Dr. Ricardo took out the remaining tiny piece with his hands.

Cost in money—nothing for me and little for the clinic. Cost in time? Less than thirty minutes. In too many cases, the United States is using expensive machinery when two "hands-on" hands would be more useful.

Are there problems with Mexican health care delivery? *Seguro Popular*, the national "people's insurance" that covers many of Mexico's poorest 50 million, can be frustrating and time-consuming for nonthreatening illnesses. But when the illness is serious, the care is excellent. When a friend's ten-year-old nephew was diagnosed with a rare intestinal cancer, we asked a US doctor to assess his treatment program. He found it to be as sophisticated as cutting-edge US protocols.

As in every country, not every doctor is up to the task. I saw a Mexican doctor once, highly recommended, who wrote nothing during his consultation with me. He suggested blood tests and a return visit one week later, instructions that I jotted in a notebook. When I came back, he had no idea who I was.

"When were you last here?" He coughed and began rearranging the papers on his desk.

"Tuesday."

He stared hard at me. My *bienestar* wavered.

"Ah, yes," he said. "I remember you. I recognize your earrings." I feigned a smile and wrote in my notebook, *Don't let him operate.*

So it is everywhere. A friend in the United States told me that his nurses advised him to write *NOT THIS SIDE* in permanent magic marker on his right thigh when he went for left hip–replacement surgery. Health care suffers from human error the world over. And may I just say, the hospital gown is the same unfortunate fashion statement no matter what country you are in.

I glanced at my new friend on the bench. I was glad she had not realized I'd had an episode of San Miguel syndrome while we were talking about health care. She patted my leg affectionately and moved on to question number two.

"But what about the drug cartels?"

Now, *that's* a question that can really destroy *bienestar*.

RISK IS RELATIVE

I WAS DOING A HAPHAZARD survey of my San Miguel friends on safety precautions while driving in Mexico.

"Where would you hide money to keep it safe in case you were carjacked?" I asked. I was talking to a woman I had just met at a cocktail party.

She paused to consider her options before nodding firmly. "Under the floor mat in the backseat," she announced.

Excuse me? I could see she was not accustomed to thinking about how a carjacking goes down. I didn't want to inform her that her money was leaving with her car, so I pretended I had to call my mother and moved on.

What precipitated my survey was the news that a Canadian couple had recently been carjacked on a Mexican highway on their way to the beach. They were not physically harmed, but being left by the side of the road with nothing is an unpleasant prospect. Señor Roberto and I were going to the beach, and we, too, were driving. When I heard this, fear flew around my brain like metal filings to a magnet. Instead of worrying about the usual dangers of driving in Mexico—would we get lost (yes, every year), would the car break down (twice), or would we hit a bus in Guadalajara (yes, once last year) —now I could fret about carjacking.

I strategized our eight-hour trip as I reviewed safe driving tactics. Always travel in back of a line of cars, preferably including a bus, and, of course, never drive at night. The car was insured, the computers were backed up, and I would happily hand over the old clothes we'd packed to hang out at the beach. But if I had to be left by the side of the road, I wanted to do so with our money intact. Where we were going, American Express might as well be the pony express, and the nearest ATM, sixty minutes away, rarely had money. In our car, cash was riding shotgun.

My survey showed the most popular hiding places for money in case of carjacking are in a shoe or a bra. But I wear sandals and I am not satisfied with the bra solution, which might create a lumpy fashion statement. I wanted something more secure, less predictable.

Finally, I came up with an out-of-the-box idea. At dinner with friends, I revealed that despite the recent carjacking, I had no worries about carrying cash on our trip. Everyone leaned in close to hear the secret of my confidence.

"Sanitary napkins," I whispered. Eyebrows shot skyward, as if no one had heard those two words in thirty years—which, given the average age of those present, was reasonably accurate.

"I'm going to retrofit a sanitary napkin to hold my money," I announced. "No one in his right mind would look there, and these days they have adhesive for secure mounting and negative ions that relieve stress and reduce body fatigue. I'm not sure how that works, but what could be better for a long road trip?"

Ignoring certain cruel suggestions that I was beyond the age limit for possession, I bought a box. After a little light manufacturing, it was perfect. Well, not perfect. At our first bathroom stop, I noticed five 100-peso notes on the floor of the stall. I thought it was my lucky day until I realized they had fallen out of my underwear.

Extreme measures for a car trip, perhaps, but—thanks to the US media—we think a lot about the risks of living and traveling in Mexico these days. People are constantly asking, "How likely is it I will be murdered by the drug cartel if I go there?"

I have tried to answer that question—for the sixty-five people who came to Mexico for my daughter's wedding, and for the many tourists whose families ask for their life insurance information before they leave for the airport.

First, let's acknowledge what is true. Mexico has too much violence—fueled by warring drug cartels, corruption, and a weak criminal-justice system, fed by the unending supply of US guns and our unquenchable appetite for drugs. Murder, or any violent crime, regardless of where or how it occurs, is an unimaginable personal loss not answerable to any statistic. But I also tell people it is safer in most of Mexico than in much of the

United States. You are at least four times more likely to be a murder victim in St. Louis, Washington, DC, and New Orleans than you are here.

In fact, many of the US citizens who ask about being murdered here happily inhabit cities with a higher murder rate than San Miguel. Perhaps they feel safe there because they unconsciously cut their odds of violent crime by doing away with known risk factors—like not living or walking alone in high-crime neighborhoods, not consorting with drug dealers or gang members, securing their homes against forced entry, and never, ever double-crossing, criticizing, or owing money to people who carry guns.

Here's good news for the older set: being over age forty also lowers risk (maybe we're in bed before the majority of murders are committed), and being a woman does, too, since more than 78 percent of murder victims are male. I also recommend living with a nice, nonviolent person. A family member kills more than 40 percent of all female murder victims.

Eliminating just a few risk factors like these decreases the already-low odds that you will be a victim anywhere, either in your hometown or in Mexico. If you can stay away from the people, places, and situations where murder is more likely to occur (lucky you—many people in Mexico and the United States do not have that option), what is left is being in the wrong place at the wrong time, a statistical micropossibility. After all, the world is risky—cows kill twenty-two people in the United States every year.

Of course, statistics are not a guarantee; they help us to look at reality and make more rational choices. The problem is that it is our *perception* of risk, not reality, that drives our decision making. And our perception of risk is not rational. The threat of death by a terrorist attack strikes fear in our hearts, but many more people have died from patriotic fireworks on the Fourth of July. If one shark fin is sighted off the shore, the beach will be empty for the summer. Guess what? It is more likely that you will die falling from a ladder while you're cleaning out your gutter, which your wife made you do when you didn't go to the beach.

Some people who will not travel to Mexico because they are worried about dying before their time will explain this to you while smoking a cigarette, eating a Twinkie, and balancing a drink on the top of their basketball-size stomach. News flash! You are more likely to die of heart disease than to be murdered in Mexico or anywhere else in the world. Our brains are hardwired to fear first and analyze later. Sometimes, later never comes.

When I was visiting my mother, who lives near Atlantic City, New Jersey, a friend of hers commented on how brave I must be to live in a place like Mexico, where the threat of mayhem lurks around every corner. When she said it, it sounded like "brave" might be a synonym for "stupid."

"No, not really," I said. I mentioned that just the day before, the front page of her local newspaper had run a story of a couple who were carjacked leaving a parking garage in Atlantic City and then murdered. Did that worry her?

"Oh, no," she said. "That doesn't affect me. That happened fifteen miles away."

"But, see, most of the drug violence in Mexico is hundreds of miles away from where I live, almost as many as from Atlantic City to Atlanta." I was sure she would see that logic.

She narrowed her eyes and shot a suspicious glance at me. "But still," she said.

There are many reasons why certain risks irrationally frighten us more than others, and as tourists or residents in Mexico, we experience many of them—a lack of control, an element of the unknown, a heightened sensitivity when the victim is a *norteamericano* who "looks like us." Add in the brain's natural proclivity for negative rather than positive news, and it is hard to remember that the odds of being a victim of violence in Mexico are close to the odds of Señor Roberto's getting a date with a supermodel, more or less 88,000 to 1.

I have my own irrational fears—which, of course, I do not find irrational. I am not as troubled about the risk of murder in Mexico as I am about entering a bar in the twenty-two US states where people believe that their presence with a loaded weapon improves safety. People filled with fear and beer and "carrying concealed" feel dangerous to me.

But for the majority of people in the United States, dogs are more of a threat than guns, since Rover is universally banned in US food establishments. That's just wrong. If the waiter kissed my dog on the lips, rubbed his doggy bottom, and then prepared my french fries without washing his hands, I might worry about germs. But people and one-dollar bills spread many more bad microbes than dogs, and I have noticed that both are in restaurants all the time. From a risk perspective, laws can also be a bit off the mark.

I met a Canadian couple who had driven their RV from Canada south into Mexico for many years. I asked them if they were worried now.

"For sure. We are always afraid when we make this trip." They nodded in unison.

"Yes," I sympathized. "I guess it could be scary driving in Mexico."

They looked confused.

"Oh, my, no," they said, "we're not afraid of driving in Mexico. We're afraid of driving in the United States. If we get sick or get in an accident in the United States, where Canadian health insurance does not cover us, we could be bankrupted by the US health care system."

Well, yes, that's statistically more likely than being killed by sharks, dog germs, or a drug cartel.

We arrived at the beach without incident, except that when I went to plug in my computer, I discovered that I had forgotten my charger. Odds of carjacking: maybe one in ten million. Odds I would forget a charger: one in ten. Ability to focus on the wrong risk: typical.

ANNOUNCING THE WINNER OF MY PERSONAL TRAVEL CONTEST, CALLED "THE BEST UNDISCOVERED BEACH SPOT EVER"

WHEN IT COMES TO taking a beach vacation, Señor Roberto and I could not have more different views. He is a strong believer in undiscovered Mexican beach spots where the amenities are generally limited to a lumpy bed and a resident iguana. I, on the other hand, am a person who worked eighty hours a week in a high-stress environment. I rationalize beach spas as a necessity associated with the production of income, using an earned-value technique, an internal rate of return, and a cost-benefit analysis. As you might imagine, this difference in view can lead to marital discord.

When it came time to take our annual beach vacation, I went on the offensive for an all-inclusive ocean resort and spa where the only decision necessary would be whether to have the seaweed body wrap before or after an organic, locally grown vegetarian lunch, cooked and served without my participation; where I could have the Pacifica masque and mineral scrub, guaranteed to cause a profound transformation in my cellular makeup, release all my toxins, correct my tensions at the deepest level, and unblock my trapped energy.

"Think of it as the cost of doing business," I told Señor Roberto. "Think of it as something that makes it possible for me to work. Think of the cost-benefit ratio."

"Nice try," he said, "but the last I heard, you're mostly retired." And just like that, the ocean resort and spa was relegated to the loofah-lined dustbin of my former life and the undiscovered-beach-spot vacation became the new normal.

If you are thinking that I am filled with unreleased toxins and uncorrected tensions, all directed at Señor Roberto, you are right. To unblock my trapped energy, I decided to sponsor my own travel contest, hereinafter known as "The Best Undiscovered Beach Spot Ever." If I have to go to an undiscovered beach spot, I at least want to find the right one.

Let me give you the sophisticated system I will use for scoring points in my contest. I will award a maximum of ten points for each of the criteria below. Some may require deduction of points, some may be eligible for bonus points, and the whole thing is at my sole discretion. Do not write to me with your suggestions or complaints; write to Señor Roberto.

Here are the criteria:

1. The undiscovered beach spot should have nothing but beach, ocean, dirt roads, and a few stores that sell inflatable beach toys. Briny air mixed with an occasional rotting fish carcass should perfume streets with no names and no house numbers. Bonus points are allowed if you have to drive up and down every street in town to find the house you have rented, the full, complete address of which, including zip code, is "the blue house on the beach."

2. The town must have no more than twenty-five tourists, and only five can be gringos. There should be a lot of local Mexicans who cannot imagine what you are doing there but welcome you with enthusiasm and curiosity. If you can identify by name ten people in town whom you consider friends by the time you leave, you will earn ten bonus points. Getting invited to a local child's third-birthday party is worth twenty points, even if you do not want to go.

3. There can be only one restaurant in town open during the day, and then only sporadically. The one restaurant allowed must have a devil-may-care attitude about both the speed of service and the flexibility of the menu. They will not make a bacon omelet if it is not on the menu, even if they

have bacon, because the omelet is always a ham omelet. Period. No points here if there are any restaurants open at night, although taco stands are permitted. You must either come to love fried pork or cook at home. This is a difficult decision—ask your health care provider if fried pork is right for you.

4. It must be impossible—no, it must be unthinkable—to buy arugula or mesclun lettuce. Rare sightings of the iceberg kind, if it is limp, are permissible. White wine cannot be an item that is available every day; it should be seen only when the white-wine man comes from a distant town, and only then if he thinks to bring it. "Buy local" will be not so much a political statement as a statement of fact. You'll get ten bonus points if the only store has a handwritten sign with the names of the people in town whose credit has been cut off and a plastic Jesus presiding over a Coca-Cola cooler.

5. You are required to look out of open doors and see a beach that is empty except for a few stray dogs that are running, playing, digging holes in the sand, and plopping down in them. You must be able to run on the beach for at least two miles before you turn around. Occasionally you must see dolphins and whales, which will come as a surprise since you believe, as we do, that these

marvelous creatures live only in water parks. If
you see even one umbrella or beach chair, you
will receive no points for this category; I don't
care how far you run.

6. Trucks with loudspeakers roped precariously to
their roofs must be the only communication
system, informing you daily of the trash pickup
schedule and a volleyball game on the beach. You
are permitted to receive local news via a ten-year-
old boy, improbably named Brandon, who comes
over every day to tell you the gossip, lured by an
inexhaustible supply of packaged cookies accur-
ately called *Polvorónes*, which means "dry as dust."

7. The presence of a television in your *casa* imme-
diately and irrevocably disqualifies an undiscovered beach spot from the contest, but you are
permitted to have Internet access if it is constantly
interrupted because the owner of the service has
to turn it off every time he gets a phone call.
Wireless coverage must be less than an itsy-bitsy
teeny-weeny yellow-polka-dot bikini.

8. A scorpion must sting your husband when he puts
his hand in the sink, complaining that you have
not cleaned up from the last meal. While you do
not have to believe that this is proof there is a just
God, it won't hurt. You will have to go to the
local clinic for intravenous antivenom medication,

but if *la doctora* looks like Salma Hayek, the husband will not mind. Please submit the medical bills in support of this category, even if the two hours in the emergency room cost less than US$40.

9. To get points in this final category, you must find a garter snake under your pillow in the morning that looks very sleepy and doesn't seem to understand that sustained, high-pitched screaming while jumping up and down means that he needs to leave. (Note: Photographic evidence may be necessary to award points in this category. Alternatively, a signed affidavit attesting to a mental breakdown that required extensive spousal counseling on the meaning of the expression "all creatures great and small" can be accepted.)

For the real bonus, you must discover certain priceless lessons: The stock market, like the sun, rises and falls every day without your help. As cell phone reception declines, you are less inclined to speak and more inclined to listen. Organic food never goes out of style when you cannot afford pesticides. Sand is great for exfoliation; seaweed and saltwater baths are not exclusive to spas. The daily drama and hysteria of twenty-four-hour news advance fear, but simplicity remains perfect and requires no upgrade. Version 0.0 is enough. Margaritas are not required for the bonus, but they may help in correcting tensions at the deepest level.

So, those are the criteria for my contest. Now that my trapped energy is unblocked, I will announce the winner. On second thought, I had better not say. I am definitely coming back next year to see my snake, and I want this particular spot to remain undiscovered.

Where We Purchase Diego's Freedom for 140 Pesos

IN THE MURKY DAWN LIGHT, I wake to a shrill police siren, the pitiful mewing of cats, and a whippoorwill with anger management issues, followed in quick succession by the staccato screech of an alarm and the insistent ringing of a telephone. I stretch and move one toasty foot out into the cool air. I am not concerned. It sounds like the apocalypse, but these are only the early-morning musings of Diego, our resident mockingbird. He lives in a cage just outside our bedroom door.

My first "bird in a cage" experience came years before, with another Diego. (For unremembered reasons, we have named the only two birds we have had Diego, perhaps influenced by George Foreman, who named each of his sons George.) Diego arrived in our household while I was on a business trip in the United States. On my return, Señor Roberto announced that he and Luis Fernando, the cook, had purchased a surprise for me, and together, quivering with self-satisfaction, they unveiled a cage.

Ta-da! It was a cardinal. I gasped in horror. I said, "It's a cardinal!" They smiled and nodded.

"It's a wild bird!" I said. They felt they could not confirm or deny.

Luis Fernando explained how he had helped Señor Roberto select this very fine bird for me and that his role had not been merely to accompany Señor Roberto to the market—no, he had been intimately involved in the selection, in discussions with the seller, in the negotiation for the cage. Without Luis Fernando's excellent help and Señor Robert's 140 pesos, this very fine bird would not be sitting here today on this patio, in this cage.

"Oy," I said. Not the *hoy* that means "today" in Spanish, but the *oy* that means "What in the name of all that is holy am I going to do now?" in Yiddish.

It took a week of downloaded bird photographs held up in front of the cage before Señor Roberto could come to admit that, well, yes, Diego surely looked like a cardinal. I persuaded him that we had to open the cage door and let Diego go free.

Señor Roberto was not fully on board with the release strategy. "I don't think he'll leave the cage. He'll be too frightened."

When the door opened, Diego was gone faster than the human eye can register movement.

Then I had to break the news to Luis Fernando. I wanted to do this in a way that would not confer my own moral judgments or diminish his pride in the bird-buying caper.

"Mexicans keep wild birds in cages," I said carefully, "but gringos are extremely sensitive to this kind of thing, and so, because I am a gringa, I had to let the cardinal go free."

Luis Fernando shook his head vigorously in agreement. He leaned in and whispered, "*Sí, señora*, I understand. I tried to tell Señor Roberto you would not like this bird, but he would not listen to me."

Now we have Diego the mockingbird, who also lives in a cage. No creature should be in a cage, I argue with myself. But he was a gift from a Mexican friend. I don't know what to do about birds in cages, the treatment of dogs, circus animals—there are so many culture clashes here. I console myself with the knowledge that mockingbirds are kept in captivity around the world. I tell myself that after so long among humans, he couldn't fend for himself, that he needs me to provide his daily papaya. That may be true, but, even to me, it sounds like a rationalization. In reality, I love his presence—his puffed-up attitude and his vast communication skills.

Mockingbirds are musical miracles. They can imitate a multitude of sounds, stringing them together in a now rhapsodic, then atonal and confusing symphonic creation. There is a Nahuatl poem on the 100-peso note about mockingbirds, or *cenzontles*, as they are called in Spanish. It is tiny, but under a magnifying glass it is possible to read, "I love the song of the mockingbird, Bird of 400 voices . . ."

The dogs are particularly disturbed by Diego's cat

imitations. They jump up from their daylong naps on the hot terra cotta tiles, convinced there is a cat to chase—but one never appears. Diego hops excitedly on his perch, as though he enjoys his joke, as the dogs dash here and there in frenzied, barking confusion.

Diego likes music, particularly music to which he can sing along. I have a special playlist on my iPod with his favorites: the Dominican artist Hector Acosta; Mexican favorite Alejandro Fernández and his father, Vicente Fernández, especially when they sing together; and, yes, Renée Fleming. Diego does not like jazz. This is strange, because he resembles a jazz singer—all riffs, wails, sounds strung like beads on a wire; now a bird, now a siren, a whistle, an ascending scale, a staccato shriek—infinite possibilities and choices flowing effortlessly from a tiny body.

When Diego II leaves us for the great bird heaven in the sky, as he surely will someday, I will not replace him. I don't believe in putting birds in cages. But in the meantime, I provide the papaya, he provides the singing, and we have one of many US–Mexican cultural truces.

SEMANA SANTA

IT'S 10:30 A.M., and it's already eighty-five degrees. I hum "Hark! The Herald Angels Sing" as sweat trickles down my back. Perched on the ledge of a dry fountain in the main church courtyard, I watch the arrival of hundreds of angels, penitents, Roman soldiers, and musicians who on a normal day are schoolchildren, shop-keepers, plumbers, and real estate agents. They stream to the staging area for the most important religious holiday of the Mexican year: Good Friday in San Miguel de Allende.

Good Friday unspools like a four-act drama that takes a day to deliver. The Reenactment of the Trial of Jesus kicks it off, followed by the Procession of the Priest's Passing, the Sacred Encounter, and the Holy Burial Procession. Stamina, strategy, water, and sunscreen are required to make it to the end, but *vale la pena*; indeed, more than worth the pain, it is all about the pain. Today, we relive the familiar story of suffering and redemption.

But for this moment, I wait. And my mind wanders.

Behold the Angel of God. She is four years old, dark, with complicated braids, a white dress, purple sash, and handmade angel wings. Her mother's rushing hand propels her, as she is sorely late. Verily, an untold number of Angels of God are late, and the scene fairly hums with fluffy, scurrying creatures.

Act I: The Reenactment of the Trial of Jesus

From my vantage point on the fountain, I watch the man in charge of organizing the stage. Directing the setup in the entry of the old church, he resembles an energetic orchestra conductor in the fast movement of Beethoven's Seventh. His helpers dash back and forth, banging on the wooden platform, setting up the podium, the microphone, and the wooden image of Jesus.

It is now well past the advertised start time of 11:00 a.m. The hard concrete ledge is getting harder. My left brain wonders why they didn't get started setting up earlier, while my right brain says, *Whatever.* Time is an abundant resource here, and nobody in her right mind expects this to start as scheduled.

I bring out my water bottle. It is already empty.

Finally, with words from the priest, the drama begins. The same man plays Pontius Pilate every year. He looks authentic in his Roman costume, with his deep, authoritative voice and wide stance that anchors him to the stage while he delivers his lines. I can't understand everything he says, but it doesn't matter. I know the story.

After Pilate commutes Barabbas's sentence and washes his hands, the drama stops. The many stagehands dash across the stage once again. Now they dismantle the recently assembled platform and remove the podium so the procession, waiting in back, can begin. This takes time. My left brain wonders why they don't just have the trial in another place so they do not have to disassemble an entire stage while the audience waits in the heat. My right brain remembers it has been in this spot since before the United States was a country, so probably they don't need my help.

I apply more sunscreen. And I wait.

Did not your father and your father's father dismantle this very stage? Hast not your family and thou dismantled this stage for hundreds of years? I sayeth unto you, "What's the holdup?"

Act II: The Procession of the Priest's Passing

Once the stage is removed, the slow processional stream begins. Men in black pants and white shirts shoulder huge wooden platforms, adorned with flowers and life-size statues hand-carved and painted by *santeros*, or "saint makers," whose craft has existed for generations. This particular pageant began in 1756, organized by the most famous of San Miguel priests, Father Luis Felipe Neri de Alfaro, who carried a cross and was flogged by the crowd as he passed.

We hold our collective breath as the men, young and old, struggle under their heavy load, each steep, uneven stone step precarious. Soon women dressed in black and carrying similar palanquins, of Mary, Veronica, and Mary

Magdalene, will negotiate the steps in high heels. Coming now are the Angel Choir, musicians and penitents, Roman soldiers, more statues of saints, and the current parish priest with lash marks painted on his bare chest— the crowd no longer flogs him. Somber music hangs in the heat.

The procession passes. Through the churchyard and into the surrounding streets it moves, releasing the woody fragrance of the chamomile tossed in its path.

Ask and ye shall be given the Angel Choir, young and animated. Their voices are as sweet as agave syrup. Worry not that any will escape the procession. Women in black lace mantillas interrupt their fidgets with gentle touches, keeping them together.

Act III: The Sacred Encounter

The men and women carrying these weighty wooden shrines plod through the historic center. They are literally and figuratively sharing in the suffering of this day. Heat, the heavy burden, the high heels—this is a work of devotion. They stop frequently, resting their pallets on narrow hinged sawhorses that are carried and placed with the precision of a well-choreographed ballet. Every square inch of the town square is blanketed by people with raised umbrellas. They do not expect an imminent downpour; they are shielding themselves from the razor-sharp sun.

After two long, hot hours, the procession has circled back to where it began. I wait, like everyone there, to see the Sacred Encounter. I try to get a space at the top of the stairs leading to the churchyard. From this vantage point, I can better witness the moment when the wooden statue of Jesus encounters the statue of his mother, Mary—he on his way to death, she on her way to live with this memory. He approaches from the left, she from the right. He is robed in purple, body bent, dragging the cross, blood tracing his face and hands; she is robed in blue, her hands raised slightly off center, fingertips touching as in supplication.

We wait in a hush. The only sounds are those of cameras clicking and whirring like technological crickets. After seemingly endless seconds, almost imperceptibly, Jesus bows his head to his mother, Mary. Slowly. Deliberately. Three times.

This heartbreaking, human gesture has no sophisticated visual effects, no orchestrated music, dramatic lighting, or computer-generated images. This is not a James Cameron movie. It is a "homemade" event—an expression of the ordinary devotion of those who make and remake the scene every year. A *santero* made this statue of Jesus—a man whose father and grandfather before him made religious icons. Mary was made by another man whose father and grandfather before him made statues. A man under Jesus's bier pulls the rope that nods his head. These icons are tended by church members who clean and prepare them for this day with loving attention and generations of experience.

Like electricity, the sorrow flows through us. I think of Aeneas, wandering for years after the Trojan War. In

Carthage, he came upon a monument to that war's senseless tragedies. There were carvings of the Trojan women broken open in grief, scenes of Achilles dragging the body of Aeneas's friend Hector and then selling the corpse for gold. Aeneas wrote, "These men know the pathos of life, and mortal things touch their hearts."

Today, we know the "pathos of life." Our tears are for Mary, for the loss of a child, for injustice, for the devotion of Mexicans, and, perhaps, for what has been lost in our own lives.

But with the tears, there is also a sense of grace, the free, unearned gift of connection. With nothing more than three small bows of a statue's head—for just a moment, but long enough—we inhabit together a sacred space.

Blessed be the older Mexican woman who sits on the church steps in a worn cotton dress. She moves over to make room for an Anglo woman carrying an expensive camera. Their eyes meet; they nod as the mexicana *raises her umbrella to share precious shade with the other.*

The Intermission

After the Sacred Encounter, I have to go home. The heat has covered me like the fine dust of the pre–rainy season. I want some shelter, lemonade, and Kleenex to strengthen me for the remaining events of the day. I need to renew my stamina and refill my water bottle.

Act IV: The Holy Burial Procession

At 4:00 p.m., the final act of the Good Friday passion play, the Holy Burial Procession, begins with the beat of a single drum. Starting in the late afternoon, approximately 1,500 people—men and boys, women and girls—march as centurions, lantern holders, and pallbearers who carry the weight of the saints, the archangels, and Jesus and Mary. Thirty-six men in black suits bear Jesus' crucified body on a platform weighing over a ton. The cortege will last for hours.

The Roman centurions have short skirts, red knee socks, and what appear to be plastic broom bristles on the tops of their helmets. They walk to the beat of the drum— one foot down, stop. One foot down, stop. A small orchestra passes, playing sacred music in a minor key. The music, a dirge, was written for this procession by José María Dolores Correa Pérez over one hundred years ago. Where I stand at the corner of the Jardín, they stop to accompany a woman on the balcony above us as she sings hauntingly into the gathering dusk.

Sing a joyful noise unto the Lord, and fear not that the musicians will lose their notes while walking. A small boy marches ahead of them with the sheet music clipped to the back of his shirt with a clothespin.

Families take their prescribed role in this drama, as they have for centuries. Girls who begin as Angels of God grow to accept the weight and suffering of Mary, Veronica, or Mary Magdalene. The mantilla-shrouded women chaperoning Angels were once Angels themselves. Boys carry the sepulcher, and in time, following their fathers and uncles, they will hold the saints, or maybe even Jesus, on their shoulders. Time moves in a circle, the past connected to the present and the future on a knotted thread of ceremonies. As the day darkens, hundreds of lanterns blink, perforating the smudges of pink and blue sky—solemn fireflies snaking down narrow stone lanes.

Blessed is the teenage lantern carrier who is chewing gum. He goeth in a dark suit two sizes too broad in the shoulders and one size too short in the sleeves. Lo, his older brother hath a different shape.

Easter Sunday: The Aftermath

On Good Friday, San Miguel groans under the weight of suffering, but on Easter Sunday, Mexicans, those acrobats at life, bring out all the weapons necessary to vanquish the forces of evil: explosives.

This is not a day for warm-and-fuzzy Easter bunnies or chocolate eggs. Instead, the exuberant tradition of the Burning of the Judases happens all over Mexico. The Judas figures, representing evil, corruption, and betrayal, are built with reeds and papier-mâché, gasoline and dynamite, elevating the Mexican affection for fireworks and explosions to an art form. Because Mexicans love social and political satire, the Judases are often likenesses of prominent people. One of Diego Rivera's murals in the Ministry of Education in Mexico City shows the Judases as a politician, a general, and a priest, representatives of the three institutions that have long betrayed the Mexican people. But the Judases are not limited to Mexicans.

Strung high up above us in the main square, each figure twirls and twists one quarter turn, then lazily in the other direction, back again and yet again, as if evil had all the time in the world to mesmerize us, to hypnotize us, to seduce—*WHAM!* With what feels like a megaton of force, it explodes. Big papier-mâché shards rain down; children and adults scramble to get the arms and legs, maybe a head. With a bang, not a whimper, Easter ends.

And it came to pass that as the charred paper known as Bush, Obama, and others unceremoniously drifted to the ground, God said, "Be still now." But He did not mean here in Mexico, for here we shall pass many more days of noise while we wait to be redeemed again next year.

SECTION THREE

THE FACE OF POVERTY

Ojos que no ven, corazón que no siente.
"Eyes that do not see, heart that does not feel."
—MEXICAN EXPRESSION

The Face of Poverty

SHE SITS ON THE FRONT step of my house, her feet resting on the sidewalk in flat, scuffed shoes an inch too long in the heel, a plastic carryall beside her. A thin shawl is wrapped around the faded shoulders of a wash-worn cotton dress and up over her head, exposing her left eye, which is patched with gauze and ragged tape. Doña Consuelo is one of twenty-two million Mexicans who are the face of the extreme poor.

When we first moved into our newly remodeled home, called Cinco Flores, a haven of art, plants, and light, I came out of the front door and nearly tripped over this woman begging. While the United States has its share of poverty, it does not sit on middle-class doorsteps. I did not want to see her face.

"Why does this homeless-looking street person sit at my house?" I railed. "Why can't she sit somewhere else, instead of on my front step? Why doesn't she get a job?" Luckily, I lacked the Spanish vocabulary to know how, or to whom, to express my ignorance.

The most recent statistics on poverty in Mexico report that fifty-three million people, close to 46 percent of the population, are classified as poor. Poverty is further divided into subgroups like the "extreme poor" and the "moderately poor." This is determined not just by income but also by a multidimensional measurement based on ability to access food, health care, education, housing, and other necessary services. Add in those who are vulnerable to becoming poor because they lack access to one or more of these services, or because they are very close to the poverty line, and it is estimated that the number of Mexico's poor soars to an astronomical 80 percent.

Extreme poverty is a legacy of birth in this static, class-frozen society. The extreme poor, like Doña Consuelo who sits on my step, often live in rural areas on less than US$53 a month. Poor health, hunger, dirt floors, cardboard roofs, and a lack of electricity and plumbing are their inheritance. They sit on the streets and beg, make a few tortillas, or pick wildflowers to sell.

The "moderately poor" have jobs, but they are often in Mexico's informal economy: no taxes, no regulation, no banking—a place where resourcefulness keeps them in business. This underground financial system, estimated to include 30 percent of Mexican workers, is driven by ingenuity and a variety of wheels. Wheels propel a rusted shopping cart filled with oranges, a hand juicer bolted to a board wobbling on top; a bicyclist moves through cobbled streets, a knife sharpener attached to a rear wheel; a junk dealer collects scrap metal, plastic, and glass in a pushcart. These one- or two-person enterprises provide bare subsistence for families and cannot grow because, like approximately 94 percent of Mexican businesses, they lack access to credit or capital.

Moderately poor people may also be employed in Mexico's formal economy, where the minimum wage is fifty-seven pesos per day (US$4.30 at the exchange rate at the time of this book's publication) but where they may be eligible for social services like health care and a small retirement income. No matter where they are working, these are the working poor—all 30 million of them.

While our home was being remodeled, we often ate in a modest neighborhood restaurant where there were only eight tables. As we enjoyed wine and *cervezas*, enchiladas or *gringas* (tortillas stuffed with savory fried pork), a tiny old man, his face wrinkled and caved in on itself, came in with his guitar, pulled out a chair, and played. After a few halting, off-key songs, he went around from table to table, his hand outstretched for money. I averted my eyes when I heard him play. I cringed when I saw him coming. I wondered why the owner would allow these uncomfortable episodes to happen. Then I noticed how the middle-class Mexicans, almost to a person, treated him with tremendous respect as they greeted him, looked him in the eyes, and handed over a few coins, or sometimes the food from their table.

I was shamed.

Mexican generosity is stunning. A friend told me about her housekeeper, Rosa, who lives with her family near the train tracks where many desperate Central Americans stop on their way to cross the US border illegally. Rosa opened her door and her home one cold, rainy night to a woman with a baby boy seeking refuge. To our US middle-class eyes, this family has nothing extra to share, but share they did. In the early morning, the woman was gone but the baby remained.

Questions overwhelm me. Why would a woman abandon her child? Did she believe that because the journey was dangerous, he might be safer with others? Because she knew that a family who would take them in and feed them, even if only for a night, were good people who would find a home for the baby or care for him themselves?

Then I have to ask myself: Would I have opened my door? Or would I have been afraid of getting involved, suspicious of her motives? Would I have cared for the baby left behind?

Rosa and her family kept the baby and raised him as their own. "God brought him to us," her husband said —"how could we say no?" A man who drove a truck selling gas helped them to secure a legal adoption, an expensive and arduous process in the best of circumstances. I am not a sociologist, an anthropologist, or an economist, but what I observe here is that those who live amid this poverty, including the poor themselves, are more generous than those of us with means but whose homes, schools, and lives are subtly and not so subtly segregated from it. We can talk about poverty—we may

even hold liberal political or religious be
poverty—but that does not necessarily make
generous. To do that, we have to see poverty's face.

Once we see it, we change. Here in San Miguel, the
hearts of most foreigners, individually and collectively, are
large, as if we have been together in a fire that has cracked
us open and made us into seeds for change. Dogs get
sterilized, adopted, and taken off the streets, and children
who come to school hungry get fed. Scholarships
materialize for bright young people with no other
opportunity to go to university. There is almost no one
whose needs are not the focus of an effort to make things
better. It is true that foreigners here raise prices and crowd
Mexicans out of housing. Our loud voices carry strong
opinions and weak understanding of Mexican history and
culture. But our being here often makes us more
generous.

Despite my good intentions, I cannot escape the
ambiguity I experience living amid this endless need. In
theory I am sympathetic, but in practice I am often
irritated by the constant interruption of vendors selling
dolls, music, and baskets at every outdoor café. I am
exasperated by small children who should be in school but
who sell Chiclets in the Jardín and by beggar women
who carry babies rumored to be rented to create
sympathy among tourists. I do not know when to give
and when not to, when to give more and when less.
There are no easy answers.

In the meantime, Doña Consuelo and I bond. I buy

her wilted wildflowers, supply ibuprofen for her arthritic knees (an occupational hazard of begging), and transfer *sobras*, leftovers, from my refrigerator to her plastic carryall. While I delight in the magic, the surreal, and the humorous adventures that I have here, my eyes must see and my heart must feel the other side of Mexico, without which a full picture of this country cannot be painted.

Perhaps I am just another gringa to Doña Consuelo, but to me she is a reminder that when I walk out my front door, if I want to feel the heart of Mexico, I need to see her face.

Small Things Make Big Differences, or How Juan Pablo Got Hot Water

LATE IN THE DAY, an invisible cloud of heat gathered. I downed ice water under the shade of an umbrella while shimmering air currents rose from the scorched patio tiles and searched the sky for rain clouds. Plants watered earlier, in the cool of the morning, now looked withered, their defeated leaves drooping like the parched tongues of travelers lost in the desert. May is the cruelest month, a month of oven-dry heat and dust, here in San Miguel de Allende.

"Carol, can you come here?" Señor Roberto was at his desk, talking to our gardener. "Juan Pablo wants to borrow fifty pesos against his salary." The Bank of Cinco Flores (hereinafter known as "The Bank") was open for business.

I was a reluctant draftee into the world of employee banking services. Actually, "kicking and screaming" are the words that come to mind. It seemed paternalistic to me, a mixing of personal and business, and therefore a bad idea.

The first time one of our workers asked for an advance against salary, I was happy to give it. By the third time, I had turned moralistic.

"For heaven's sake," I said, "why don't they plan better? I am not a bank!" But, apparently, I was.

There were two good reasons why Señor Roberto and I formed a bank. The first is that domestic employees work hard but have almost no access to banking and credit—a situation that has a negative impact on their lives. The second is that domestic workers here have a concept of "care" that is above and beyond their title of housekeeper, maid, or gardener—a situation that has a positive impact on our lives. When a friend became ill, her one-day-a-week housekeeper appeared at the hospital, carrying her personal items, stayed there with her for days, paid her bills, cooked, and fed her. These people brought something so valuable to us; could we not do something that made their life easier? Could we not act like a bank?

Our initial mission was simple: "to loan money to worthy people and causes." We thought that was Luis Fernando, our cook; Magali, our housekeeper; and our gardener-handyman, Juan Pablo. But then, too soon, we learned the painful lesson of the three most frightening words in Spanish: *tengo un primo*. "I have a cousin" might not sound alarming to you, but everyone here has hundreds of cousins, most of them are worthy, and more than a few need money.

The problem with these worthy people is that no

bank worth its auditors would deem any one of them credit-worthy. They have no credit history because they have never had "credit." That means no loans, no credit or ATM cards, no borrowing for a car or a house. And interest rates? When banks will not lend to the majority of the population, "cash shops" fill the gaps, and their rate is 8 percent. No, not per year—per month. The Bank of Cinco Flores does not charge interest. That is one of the ways you can tell it is not a real bank.

The Bank lurched forward until it found itself drowning in an ocean of misunderstandings, paperwork, and cousins. Faced with collapse, we tightened up the mission statement. Now, the front cover of the tattered paper notebook where we record transactions says, "Loans are for life-changing opportunities when the possibility of repayment seems clear." These criteria are only marginally easier to manage. When resources are limited, an amazing number of spending opportunities present themselves as life-changing.

I could see that Juan Pablo was a worthy person. He smiled with enough wattage to light a small town. He was twenty-eight years old, with a wife and two young daughters. They lived in the *campo*, where people own the land, thanks to the Revolution of 1910, but many have not, in the century since, made enough progress to build decent shelter. Houses with dirt floors, cardboard walls stuffed with rags where they meet corrugated metal roofs, dot the landscape, resembling rotted teeth in a rough mouth. Juan Pablo was smart, hardworking, and resourceful, and on his land, *paso a paso*, brick by brick, he had built a modest but sturdy house.

We met Juan Pablo when he joined the crew that painted the interior of our apartments. Every day, I noticed his smile, a smile that was not only full and genuine but also given without hesitation. A bright smile is common here—it makes me think that money and happiness have a limited correlation (a proposition that scientific study is proving to be true). Juan Pablo worked for the head painter, *el maestro*, a frustrated artist who approached the walls of the house as a substitute for the canvas.

The *maestro* said, "I see this wall as a bright *amarillo*, with dark tones under the yellow to bring down the color. I see it will be beautiful in the afternoon when the sun comes to it." Painters rag-rubbed the concrete walls and applied colors with the precision of artists. Then they did it again with different colors, and when the sun came to the wall, it was indeed beautiful.

Unfortunately, the *maestro* drank away most of the money we gave him for painting because his wife took issue with his drinking and filed for divorce. He gave the rest of our money to his lawyer and did not pay the workers. We learned this when he came to work drunk, fell into a stupor, and was unceremoniously carried home. I tried not to be judgmental; tequila did that to me. Once.

We paid the workers and reduced the crew to the two men we could supervise. Juan Pablo has been here ever since, bringing an aptitude not just for painting but also for fixing anything broken. Have an iPod dock with Bose speakers that spit out static instead of music? Juan Pablo can fix it, although he doesn't know what it is. Have a coffeemaker that hisses because the water doesn't drip into the filter? Don't throw it away. He can fix it, even though he doesn't own a coffeemaker.

Juan Pablo is among Mexico's 30 million working poor. In our cheerful "village," we have three employees. Poverty comes to work every day. It pursues people relentlessly: health problems, lack of education, no capital, and an impenetrable bureaucracy legendary for its disdain toward those it should serve. Whether someone is registering a birth or opening a small business, government encounters have more layers than a strudel, taking reams of paper and precious time from those who work the hardest for the least. Those with money can bribe their way around these obstacles. The estimated $2 billion spent to grease those red-taped wheels is more than Mexico spends on its federal judiciary.

Back at The Bank, I asked Juan Pablo why he needed the money. I wanted to know if there was a "life-changing opportunity" somewhere in there.

"I need to buy water." He bought it, he told us, from a truck plying the dirt roads of the *campo*. The weather weighed hot and dry on his baby and six-year-old; his wife counted on him to return home with fifty pesos he didn't have to get a small amount of water.

Buying water from a truck? We knew nothing of this.

"How much does this water cost?"

"One thousand pesos a month." This was a meaningful percentage of his income—an example of how expensive it is to be poor.

Señor Roberto frowned. "How much does it cost to hook up to city water?"

"Either twelve thousand pesos or thirty-five hundred pesos."

This is a wide price range, especially for a bank.

"What is the difference between the twelve thousand–peso hookup and the thirty-five hundred–peso hookup?"

"For twelve thousand pesos, the city workers come out one day to dig the trench and hook up the water pipes, and I pay the city. For thirty-five hundred pesos, the same men come out at night, I help them dig the trench, they hook up the water pipes, and I pay them."

This "midnight service system" is very popular in Mexico. When the cable repairmen came to our house, they noticed we did not have "premium" service. They offered to come that night to install a black box that would allow us to circumvent the cable company, also known as their employer, and get upgraded channels without the benefit of payment.

We said, "*Gracias, pero no,*" but the issue is complicated. In a country where most utilities are regarded as ineffective, inefficient, and corrupt, Mexicans feel a certain justice in doing whatever is necessary to avoid payment, including the rampant use of *diablitos*, devices that spin the electric meter backward and steal more than

30 billion pesos' worth of electricity each year. While I have great admiration for the resourcefulness of *diablitos*, I have declined repeated offers to install one at my house. Time in a Mexican prison is a Spanish-language immersion experience I can afford to miss.

"Why don't you just pay for the thirty-five hundred-peso hookup? In less than four months, you will pay it off and save one thousand pesos each month." I thought I knew the answer, but I wanted to confirm it: he didn't have 3,500 pesos, and he had no way to save it and nowhere to borrow it from.

I could have looked away under the theory that these folks were just employees. During my career in the United States, I managed many people and never once felt responsible for their water. I had tried to do that here. But here, reality was more complicated. I was inspired by our fellow expats who helped housekeepers and gardeners find more work and keep children in school—kind souls who begged for supplies, money, an opportunity, a chance. One entrepreneurial friend had even given his house-keeper's son a camera, taught him to use it, hung his photographs on his patio, and invited his friends to come and buy them. Which they did.

Like most of our countrymen, Robert and I regularly contributed to charities in the United States but didn't often get our hands dirty. The pressures of work and raising children kept us so focused on the needs of those inside our own small spotlight, we did not see outside that brightly lit circle.

But here, like Mexican families, we help because we have a personal connection with hardship. It sits on our front steps; it enters our home. Here, where the safety net has big holes, where poverty is so rampant that it is not a crime to be poor, small things can make big differences. Simple contact makes us a congregation of believers in the interconnection of humanity where no one is "other," where we find ourselves daily asking, "How can I help?"

And so it was that, with The Bank, I found myself like other expats, each of us in our own way repaying the favor of living here.

You did not have to be a real banker to see that Juan Pablo could repay a loan from the money he saved by not buying water from the truck. But like many of his countrymen, he could never have gotten a loan from a real bank, at least not in Mexico. He had no credit because he did not have a credit card or a bank account, even though he owned a house without a mortgage, and had a steady job.

Fortunately, The Bank was not a real bank. We opened a savings account for Juan Pablo that day. Señor Roberto made a site visit to assess the need. He saw that Juan Pablo had no water but he did have hope: when he built his house, he provided for sinks in the kitchen and the bathroom, and constructed a rough shower. There were no faucets, no pipes, but the holes to contain them were there, ready, waiting, speaking clearly: *Ojalá, someday, there will be water for this family.*

Over the next several months, through a "direct

deposit" from salary, Juan Pablo saved half of the money to connect to water. Once he had that, The Bank lent him the rest. Promoting long-term savings, and then loaning small amounts of capital that can be repaid, means the money stretches further and everyone has a stake in the outcome.

At first, the water came only to an outdoor faucet, but Juan Pablo was thrilled because he had water and more income. With another small loan, Juan Pablo brought the water inside.

It is not world peace. But it defies the imagination that anyone could manage a decent life and raise children without running water. Poverty drowns people in so much adversity.

A few months later, our local meditation center discovered that its hot-water heater was shooting out flames—a state of affairs even Buddhist meditators found distracting. On Friday afternoon, Señor Roberto sent Juan Pablo to install a new one and to dispose of the old, flame-throwing model. Would we mind, asked Juan Pablo, if he took it?

Monday morning, Juan Pablo came into work with extra wattage in his smile. The old hot-water heater? He had hauled it home and repaired it for 300 pesos (US$28). Now, for the first time in his life, he had running water inside his house and the water was hot.

Later, much later, we will be invited to share many fiestas with Juan Pablo and his family. His daughters, Natalie and Carla, will be flower girls in our daughter,

Jessica's, Mexican wedding. We will sponsor cakes for third birthdays, confirmations, and first communions. We will find a used computer so that maybe his girls can swim upstream, out of poverty. Relationship banking will be frustrating, but—then again—satisfying.

The last time we were at Juan Pablo's house, we admired the recently installed tile and the patio filled with birds and succulent plants. We admired the ingenuity with which he had finished his bathroom and kitchen floors. As I balanced a paper plate on my lap, my plastic spoon took a swan dive into the garden and I headed over to the sink to rinse it. When I opened the tap, I looked across the room at Señor Roberto and he looked back at me. And in that small, shared moment, with a slight nod, we admired the hot water.

CHANGE WE DON'T WANT

THE MARKET IS JAMMED with merchants surrounded by a chaotic profusion of produce. Crimson strawberries introduce the orange-green ombré of mangoes that make way for the more flamboyant greens—limes, chayote, pepinos, tomatillos, and broccoli. A staggering array of chiles, piñatas, and flowers entices the eyes of those who make their way through the crowded corridors, while air perfumed with the pungent smell of charring meat entices the appetite. Woven plastic bags with Frida Kahlo's image peer from the ceiling around the corner from the shrine of the Virgin of Guadalupe, who guards the entrance. Commerce thrums like a well-oiled machine.

Living in Mexico makes it easy to be charmed, not by opulence and perfection but by color and chaos. I am new here, but I cannot imagine ever tiring of the vibrant sense of living life in the moment that plays out here.

"*¿Qué va a llevar, señora?*" a spindly legged, wrinkled woman intones as she flourishes her arm toward her wares just inside the door. "What will you have today?"

This place calls to me just as the merchants do, the building bristling as people navigate narrow aisles, examining beans and tomatoes, procuring food for their family meals. I smile with satisfaction as I pass. I experience a giddy sense of freedom when I am *en la calle*, doing simple errands, connecting with others doing the same. I bow my head to the Virgin of Guadalupe stationed out front, not because I am Catholic but because she is the patron saint of the Mexican people. It's a big job.

Today I am in a hurry to get home, but I need three avocados and can't resist the opportunity to enter.

In Mexico, where they produce over a million metric tons of these buttery berries, there are two categories of avocados: *hoy*, meaning "ripe enough for today," and *mañana*, "ready for another day." I stop to buy three *mañana aguacates* from one of the stalls closest to the door.

"*¿No tiene los quince pesos?*" the young clerk asks me with a worried look as I hand her a twenty-peso note.

"I don't have it, *señorita*." I show her a five-peso coin and the twenty-peso note.

The sun burns hot and strong outside, but a sense of foreboding creeps over me. My breathing quickens and my clammy hands grip a rough wooden tomato crate for support as I rock back on my heels. I am headed into a surreal twilight zone, minus the Rod Serling theme song: a slow-motion dreamscape in which the money is extended in my outstretched hand; the clerk has the avocados ready and waiting in a plastic bag; I reach for them; they hang so close. But there is a problem. She has no change.

Years ago, there was a *Saturday Night Live* parody for a business called the First Citiwide Change Bank. The Change Bank did only one financial transaction: it made change. Its motto was "We are not going to give you change you don't want." Its "commercial" said, "If you have a fifty-dollar bill, we can give you fifty singles. We can give you forty-nine singles and ten dimes. We can give you twenty-five twos. Come talk to us . . . If you come to us with a hundred-dollar bill, we're not going to give you two thousand nickels—unless that meets your particular change needs." Every time Robert and I got change—pennies, nickels, dimes—we looked at each other, laughing and chanting, "Change we don't want." In Mexico, we have the opposite of the Change Bank— we have the No-Change Bank, whose motto is "We don't make change because we don't have any."

In the market, I glance at my watch and review the possibilities as we begin the Search for Change. My clerk can: 1) find someone else willing to give her change—a painfully slow exercise, since the other merchants don't have change either; 2) offer me the avocados for five pesos and lose ten pesos; 3) not sell them, missing the whole sale; 4) take the five pesos and ask me to return someday with the rest of the money; or 5) persuade me to buy another avocado to get closer to the twenty pesos. This is complicated math for three avocados.

"*Un momentito.*" The clerk turns around and heads

toward the back of the building. Hope for a quick trip fades as avocados and pesos are held in limbo. *Un momentito* does not mean "one little moment." No, I have been here long enough to know it means, "I will wander off in the Search for Change until I can find another merchant who can give me some of theirs."

I bite the inside of my cheek and frown. I usually carry change with me at the market, but this was an unplanned trip—so, no change. My avocados will be *hoy* before *mañana*.

Finally back at home, I find that charm has dissolved and hardened into challenge. I rant, I rave, I gnash my teeth.

"Who runs a business and doesn't keep change? Who doesn't have forty cents in change?"

Once I got tired of being irritated, which took months, I cornered a friend, a US economist with expertise in Mexican economic matters.

"Jeff," I said, "are there not enough coins in circulation? Is it a problem with the Central Bank? Why can't the small businesses make change?"

Looking at me as though even a GPS couldn't guide me out of my confusion, he said, "They don't have money for change."

No money for change? My mind twirled as I began to grasp the economics. When the shopkeeper sells his product, he makes choices at the end of the day. He needs to take his meager profit, buy today's food, and pay for the bus and maybe a small bill, in cash, in person, without a bank. He does not have enough money to invest in change. Depending on his cash flow, he may barely have the money to replace what he sold.

In the same market, I once shopped for a large plastic container to hold drinks. I wanted two; there was one.

"Will you be getting another?" I asked.

"*Sí, señora, mañana.*"

I went back three times on three different *mañanas* before I discovered two challenging facts: *mañana* is not tomorrow, and either he or his supplier, or both of them, did not have the money to buy another, even though I was a ready buyer. Poverty breeds short-term thinking, and the short term often spans a single day. Mexicans are not lazy or inept at business. They are actually tremendously resourceful. It is that it is expensive to be poor.

The Mexican relationship to change is different from how it is in the United States, where over $4.077 trillion was spent via consumer and commercial credit, debit, and prepaid cards in 2013. Who needs change? In Mexico, the largest businesses take credit cards, but in a small town, most business are small businesses, and the responsibility for change falls on the buyer rather than the seller.

I learned this when I needed to rent chairs and tables for a party. I called and asked for them to be delivered.

"How much will the total be?" I asked.

"I cannot say, *señora*. Only the *jefe*, the boss, can tell you, and he is not here." This was pronounced in a tone of voice that suggested a request for classified state secrets, not for two card tables and six folding chairs. Mexican businesses are hierarchical, and employees who speak on the telephone often lack the most basic details, like pricing. Many workers in a small business are young family members, and the *jefe* is often a father, uncle, or brother-in-law, a *padrino* or godfather—in other words, in a position of respect and power that does not call for information sharing.

When the young man came with the tables and chairs and presented the receipt for seventy pesos, I, of course, could not dig up the exact amount. And, he, *por supuesto*, could not put together the necessary change. Since the man was coming back to pick them up the next day, Señor Roberto entered the fray, suggesting we could pay him then.

"No, *señor*, I cannot do that. The *jefe* says I must get the money now."

Faced with this impasse and needing the tables and chairs, we hit the streets, active participants in the Search for Change. We circled around innocent pedestrians like fruit flies on brown bananas. Aggravation having passed into apoplexy, Señor Roberto finally delivered the required exact amount.

"Why come with this delivery and not bring change?" he said. The vein on his left temple jumped.

The young man paused, drawing himself up as he took in an indignant breath.

"Because, *señor*, I do not know you will not have the change. You are the one who does not produce the payment in the right amount."

That stopped me in my tracks. The contents of my mind dropped like an overturned purse, scattering across the ground. From that now-empty space, a chiding voice reminded me, *Hello, you live in a foreign country. This is a different culture, not a southern extension of the United States where they happen to speak Spanish. This is Mexico. Expand your mind, Miss Why Don't You Have the Change?*

With this quarter-turn of the kaleidoscope, old thought patterns turned into new ones, with a different, but just as lovely, symmetry.

The No-Change Bank mentality insinuated itself into the framework of my life. In the United States, we gave change away. We tossed the undesirable change, the "change we don't want"—those small coins that dragged us down with their excess weight—into a big glass jar. We left pennies in the "give a penny, take a penny" cup at checkout. We were drowning in change.

No more. When I go into a big Mexican store, a place likely to have change, I break a large note so I can hoard the small bills and coins. Of course, the cashier knows this. So when I try to pay for a five-peso item with a 100-peso bill, she hands it back to me. "Don't you have the change?" She narrows her eyes and stares at me.

I stand firm, with the tenacity of a bird clinging to a slender branch in a gale-force wind. "*¿Cambio?* Oh, no, *señorita*, no change." I adopt a blank look.

The *señorita* may stretch on tiptoes and lean over the counter, peering into my bag to spot any coins. But I hold out my purse to show there is nothing smaller, because I carry change, like any valuable item, in a hidden location known only to me, cushioned to avoid any "giveaway" jangling. In time, she relents and gives me change.

In English, as in Spanish, "change" has a double meaning. In the United States, we may be drowning in change, but it is change we don't want. Monied interests at the top strangle the middle class, as the rungs on the ladder of upward mobility grow farther apart. In Mexico, we are hoarding change in every sense of the word. Little more than rocking-horse progress has been made against classism, racism, the gap between the rich and the poor. We see growth in the middle, but so little, so slowly. Mexico has gaping historical and economic wounds. Until children go to school instead of work, until the bottom is lifted by any rising tide of prosperity, until there is a rule of law, it's small change.

But for all the lack of advancement on Mexican social and economic issues, I am happy Mexico does not subscribe to many of the changes currently known as progress up north. I do not want to buy fruit with a sticker on it. The hard clamshell plastic packages that need a machete and nine minutes to open give me wrap rage. I don't miss the Great American Antibacterial and Germ War that requires sanitizing after touching a grocery cart. And please, save me from a more complicated television remote.

For me, dogs lying at the feet of their people in a restaurant do not cause panic, and having children running helter-skelter through our public square is healthier than scripted playdates. I may not be ready to drink unpasteurized milk, but I like seeing the pickup truck with big metal canisters and the kid in the back with his ladle. When a distinctive horn toot announces its impeding arrival, people emerge to fill their containers in the company of their neighbors. It feels more nourishing than the many-layered plastics of grocery stores.

It's all about change. Mexico does not have enough money to make change; the United States has too much money to want change. I bet two thousand nickels that everyone will get change they don't want.

Hard Work

IN A KITSCHY TOURIST SHOP, I pick up a coffee mug with a colorful image of a man above bold black letters spelling out MÉXICO. I put on my glasses to look more closely at the iconic image.

The man is leaning back, body slack against a giant cactus, wearing a coarse cotton shirt and pants, sombrero tilted to shade his face. He is a *campesino*, a *peon*, the cartoon representation of the shiftless Mexican, one of the ugliest stereotypes of the Mexican people. He is having a siesta.

In Mexico, there are people who rest and nap during the hottest time of the day. In part, the siesta is cultural, a tradition brought by the Spaniards. But it is also driven by the weather—countless Mexicans live and work where the temperature and the relative humidity match at one hundred. For Mexicans who work, eat, and sleep in unremitting *calor*, taking a break during the shimmering afternoon heat is not laziness. It is smart.

"Do you want the mug?" inquires the saleswoman.

"*Gracias, pero no.*"

I want to scold her for displaying and selling a false image of Mexican reality. But I bite my tongue. She works long hours for little money, proving the inaccuracy of the stereotype.

In truth, it is I who need the scolding. I see people every day who live with little and I make assumptions about who they are and what they should do or haven't done to improve their lives. I have no idea of the limitations they face, how the smallest things become insurmountable barriers, the weight of the deck stacked against them.

"¿QUIERE QUESO HOY, SEÑORA?"

I hear her before I see her.

Estela is as squat as a bush, her dark hair pulled back under a baseball cap with a few grayish wisps escaping from the sides. She calls out to me in a sharp voice that stings like a needle. She comes on Tuesday mornings, selling fresh cheese, carrying a Styrofoam cooler door-to-door. I am one of the first doors on her route.

The meager selection, *panela* and *ranchero*, is home-made by her cousins in their tiny village. I do not like the cheese, and I worry that the milk is not pasteurized. It has a mild flavor, but within days it converts to the faint smell of ammonia. I am puzzled by the small amount of cheese she carries. Why not sell more? Estela is poor. If she sold more cheese, she might have a better life. And why not cheddar or manchego? Why not expand the choices?

From my stairs, I look down on her upturned, squinting face.

"Not today, Estela, *muchas gracias*. Maybe next week."

"*Bueno, señora.*" She smiles, but her eyes do not agree.

MANY MEXICANS DO NOT earn enough to survive with one job, so they work two or three, from sunup until sundown, six or more days a week. Many put their lives in danger and leave their families just to get work. Does a lazy person do that?

María, who came to us looking for work, had left Mexico for the United States back in the 1990s for the same reason many Mexicans cross the border—she needed money. Not to buy a television or a smartphone, but because her youngest son had fallen from the roof of their house and required therapy, nutrition, and care she and her husband could not give. They lived in *obra Negra*, a shack with a corrugated roof and not much else—no water, no electricity, and no bathroom. They did not have enough income to meet their basic survival needs. María decided to cross the border, work illegally, and send her money back to pay for the care of their son and the materials to build a sturdier house.

María paid a *coyote*, a human smuggler, and made several failed attempts to cross that invisible line from Matamoros into Brownsville. Eventually, she succeeded.

She found two jobs, worked seven days a week, and

sent her money home. When she got a job in a Texas high school cafeteria, the principal knew her papers were fake, but he told her no one he hired from the United States lasted more than a week. The work was hot, hard, heavy, but to María it was heaven. She earned more in one week than she had in a month in Mexico. She contributed to Social Security, from which she will never collect. She paid taxes but did not collect welfare or unemployment. She worked there in that same hot, hard, heavy job for twelve years.

Does a lazy person do that?

THE POOR AND WORKING POOR, by some estimates more than 60 percent of the Mexican population, are not trying to get ahead—to land a promotion, to move into another economic or social class. These Mexicans are where they are in society by birth, skin color, caste, class, and hierarchies as old as the conquest, and that is where they will stay. Poverty has a longer shelf life than plutonium. Years of experience have written that script.

This is not so different from the United States. We speak lovingly of our upward-mobility opportunities, but research suggests that is largely a myth. In 1962, political scientist Michael Harrington wrote that most people who are poor simply "made the mistake of being born to the wrong parents." More than fifty years later, that is still true. Sixty-five percent of people born onto the lowest rungs of the ladder stay there.

The rare cases of upward mobility in Mexico require enormous sacrifices, not all of which are financial. A friend's gardener in a rural town worked to send his sons to university, not completely understanding that his children would be forced to move away, both physically and psychologically, to make the investment worthwhile. Leaving the family is an abandonment that goes against what Mexicans value most: the relationships that sustain them when all else fails. It is hard and painful, a Hobson's choice.

When Mexicans have the good fortune to be able to support themselves and their families, often by a standard that looks poor to us, they do not necessarily aspire to more. The front seat of an old pickup truck may serve as a sofa in a Mexican living room; few are working harder to replace it with something better looking, as we in the developed world might.

But I ask myself, what have we developed? A resource-rich environment and stunning technological advances, certainly. But peace of mind? Enjoyment of life? The US gross domestic product is thirteen times bigger than Mexico's, but we are trailing Mexico on every scale that measures happiness. Perhaps the 19th-century preacher Charles Spurgeon was right when he said, "If you are not content with what you have, you would not be satisfied if it were doubled." Mexicans are culturally more content with what they have.

THE CAR STRAINS AGAINST a rutted, uphill dirt road. We are going to see the "chicken lady." She sells fresh chickens in a Pacific coast village. We rush because we are late—she closes at 2:00 p.m. and often runs out of chicken by noon. We arrive at the door of her simple home in a cloud of dust and high hopes. Señor Roberto hops out to knock on her door.

"*¿Tiene pollo hoy?*" I hear his hopeful tone through the open car window.

"*No, señor. Se acabó.*"

This puzzles me. If you sell out every day, why not increase your stock so you can sell more? I make mental plans to discuss this with the chicken lady, magnanimously offer her my expertise as a person from an advanced nation to improve her business. I think of bank loans to buy more chickens, advertising campaigns, longer hours. Then, when we come rushing up at 1:45 p.m., we can buy a chicken.

From the car, I look over to the chicken lady's side yard, lush with palms and shade trees, where an older man reclines in a hammock and children play in the dirt. The chicken lady has returned from breaking Señor Roberto's heart, and she is putting a steaming pot on a battered wooden table with four unmatched legs.

Before I can build a new, technologically advanced chicken-processing plant, Señor Roberto gets back into the car.

"We could help her expand her inventory of chickens, eliminate barriers to sale, drive demand, and increase income. What do you think is the best thing to do?"

Señor Roberto pauses as he backs the car down the dirt track.

"Come earlier tomorrow."

ALL OVER MEXICO, large families live together and run small businesses, sharing expenses and earnings. If a house has a garage on the street, it can be a car wash during the day and a taco stand at night. Any narrow entryway is a juice bar or a *tiendita* offering a humble array of necessities for sale. "*Mexicanada.*" My carpenter laughs proudly as he shows me the typically Mexican way in which he has refitted a used oil drum to burn sawdust for cooking beans. *México nada*, I think, misunderstanding the word, the ability Mexicans have to make something out of *nada*, nothing.

LUPE'S TINY RESTAURANT HAS six tables filled to overflowing. I sit watching her two young sons run up to the kitchen door, carrying a plastic bag with three or four bottles of mineral water. A little later, I see them with a bottle of tequila. Limes, tortillas, dish soap, and other mysterious bags follow over the course of our ninety-minute meal. I begin to wonder if Lupe is pathologically disorganized. Who waits to buy what she needs until the middle of the evening rush?

Three decades ago, the Japanese were hailed for popularizing just-in-time (JIT), a manufacturing inventory system. Factories bought what they needed only when they needed it and saved millions. Lupe, like most small-business owners, runs a JIT restaurant, not because she knows of or admires Japanese efficiency but because she has no capital to invest in food and drink in advance of sales. So while Lupe may not know the term "supply chain," she has a good one. With cheap labor—nothing is much cheaper than your own sons—and a 150-square-foot neighborhood store giving credit until tomorrow, the process works, even without a computerized, point-of-sale ordering system or an online method for inventory management.

While many aid organizations want to teach people in underdeveloped countries like Mexico how to be entrepreneurial, my experience is the reverse: it is we, the resource-rich, who could use the lesson.

A 2011 STUDY BY THE Organisation for Economic Co-operation and Development shows that Mexicans work more than any of the world's twenty-nine advanced economies. Mexicans worked 595 minutes a day, just short of ten hours. Japan weighed in at 540 minutes, Canada at 517, and the United States at 496.

Why did Mexico score so high? Perhaps because the study included unpaid work, adding in Mexican women who toiled a whopping four hours and thirteen minutes a day in chores like cooking and cleaning. By comparison, the United States, despite a staggering number of television cooking shows, spent the least amount of time in the world on unpaid work like cooking and cleanup—a scant thirty minutes per day.

"¿QUIERE QUESO HOY, SEÑORA?"

Estela and I sit on the steps together. She tells me she lives in a tiny village an hour away by bus. She gets up at 5:00 a.m. to cook breakfast and lunch for her family before she loads her cooler with cheese and travels to far *pueblitos*. She trudges door-to-door through the dirt lanes. Estela could work in a *lonchería*, a small restaurant, right in her own village, but the hours are long for a meager 100 pesos (US$8) per day. She worries that she would not have time to care for her children. Without water and electricity, keeping children clean and fed takes time. Selling cheese is hard work, she tells me, but it earns a little more and she is home earlier to keep her family together.

She carries as much as she can and as much as the cousins are able to make—today's sales buy the milk for tomorrow's cheese. Cheddar or manchego? Unlikely. Aged cheeses can take eighteen months until sale—too many precious resources tied up for too much time.

No, it is the same *panela* and *ranchero*. I am still worried about the pasteurization. It will be more than we can eat in a week, and in a few days it will send off a faint ammonia odor.

"*Sí*, Estela. What do you have today?"

WHERE THE BANK MEETS THE *TANDA*

WHEN I STARTED PRACTICING law in a specialty known as institutional finance, a senior partner explained what it was we lawyers were doing. I had been wondering.

"Carol, our job is to keep bad things from happening to our clients." He sat behind a desk the size of a small apartment—every square inch covered with papers. Knee-high stacks of papers and files concealed the entire floor, except for a narrow path left bare so junior people like me could cross and sit in a chair opposite him. It looked to me like bad things had already happened here.

"And," he said, "if, heaven forbid, bad things do happen, our job is to make it clear who will pay." He sat, gazing out at the skyscraper views, holding his palms together and tapping his fingertips as if in impatient prayer.

I remembered this today because a woman who was going to rent from us asked why our lease did not describe what would happen to her deposit if we were visited by an earthquake and a flood. Shouldn't we add this? I had a faint recollection of my prior legal career, and I agreed.

I spent the morning sifting through old leases to find the "acts of God" clauses that would satisfy her request. While I was there, I was irresistibly drawn to include acts of sabotage, riots, terrorism, political upheaval, hurricanes, and tornadoes. Considering who pays when God behaves badly does not engender a sense of optimism and well-being.

I was testy by *la comida*, but the sheltered light and the crunchy bits of pork swimming in cumin-powered, green-chile salsa were just beginning to remind me that the world is a perfectly well-balanced place. That didn't last long.

"*¿Un coche?*" I asked. "A car?"

"Yes," Señor Roberto said. "A car."

"Magali wants to borrow money to buy a car? A machine with an engine and four wheels?"

"That's the way they usually come."

I ignored the sarcasm in favor of clarification. "Are you sure she said *coche*? I mean, *noche* sounds like *coche*. Could she want to borrow money for a night, not a car?"

But no, Señor Roberto was sure.

The reasons why this was a terrible idea lined up with the precision of Rockettes in a chorus line. Magali, our housekeeper, had no driver's license; she had never driven a car. Her sons did not have drivers' licenses. She lived within walking distance of everything in town and did not go anywhere except to Mexico City to see one of her sisters. You would have to be crazy to drive there when there are so many inexpensive and convenient buses. Or how about the fact that she couldn't afford a car? She didn't even own a refrigerator or a stove.

No, none of this made any sense. I began to feel the familiar flutter of the butterfly wings of the surreal, as if I were Alice being encouraged by the White Queen to imagine six impossible things before breakfast.

Until I moved to Mexico, I never thought much about the US banking industry, except for its recent contributions to a lot of economic pain and suffering. I have always put my money in the bank and liberated it on a regular basis with the assistance of a credit card or an ATM.

But living here, I see firsthand the contrast between even a flawed banking system and the invisible Mexican one. Most Mexicans, particularly the poor and working poor, have no banking experience. Banks can require a minimum deposit beyond their reach, or charge high fees that eat into small savings. Part of this is also cultural—in a land of informal, family businesses, banks are formal and impersonal, and many Mexicans do not trust them. Sixty-five percent of Mexicans do not use a bank.

My mind traveled back to the mission statement of The Bank ("Loans are *only* for life-changing opportunities when the possibility of repayment seems clear").

"Where would she get the money to pay back a loan for a car?" I asked Señor Roberto, deciding to focus on the possibility of repayment. Later, I could address the fact that "life-changing" probably could not technically be applied to a car that she couldn't drive.

"Her *tanda* is paying out in six weeks, and she will

have six thousand pesos [US$400]—approximately what the car costs."

"What is a *tanda?*"

"I don't know, exactly, but I think people get together and save money. We would be taking the *tanda* as collateral for six weeks."

I resolved that if we were going to take something as collateral, I needed to understand it. I wasn't an institutional finance lawyer for two years for nothing.

The first time I heard of a *tanda* was when I noticed that our cook, Luis Fernando, was humming to the radio, his movements from steaming pots to sink relaxed and breezy.

"What's up?" I asked.

"*Mi tanda* is paying today, *señora*. I will have a little extra money."

I tried to understand this *tanda*, but every question felt like an FBI interrogation into terrorist cell formation.

"*¿Una tanda tiene diez personas?* Who are these ten people?"

And, "I know it is called a *tanda* and it has ten people, but what does it do?"

Or, "*Sí*, I know it loans money and pays money, but how does it work?"

I gave up. But I understood the *tanda* in an elementary way as a big Christmas club. Remember them? When I was young, my mother had a Christmas club account at our local bank. She contributed money every week beginning in January, and then, eleven months later, in late November, she had saved enough money to buy gifts. That was before credit cards made it possible to push the payments into the future, so one could then devote the entire next year and perhaps a lifetime to paying it back.

The *tanda*, I found out, is an ingenious, collaborative mechanism providing amazing resources. With no access to saving or borrowing at a bank, many Mexicans use this flexible, communal arrangement several times a year as a way to meet their short-term financial needs.

Here's how this round-robin credit community works: If I want to start a *tanda*, it may be because a big expense is coming—perhaps, for example, I need one thousand pesos for my children's school uniforms. I cannot turn to a bank for a loan, I have no credit card or savings account, and no one I know can lend me that much money. What can I do? I can recruit others who want to save money for something—a washing machine, perhaps, a share of a niece's third-birthday party, or, yes, buying a car. I choose the term of the time commitment (say, ten weeks), the contribution (one hundred pesos a week, for example), and when I want to take my payout (often week one). In week one, I take in nine hundred pesos from my nine participants, plus my own one hundred pesos, and—*¡qué bueno!*—I have one thousand pesos to buy the school uniforms. After I take my payout, I continue to pay in one hundred pesos a week, as does everyone else. Whoever has drawn week two takes the next one thousand pesos, and on it goes. *Tandas* are flexible—they can be for shorter or longer periods of time, with higher or lower weekly contributions.

I am a recovering lawyer; I worried for a living. So my first response to the *tanda* was to fret over the person who draws week ten. What if people stop paying after they get their money? What if the *tanda* leader embezzles the money? Or it is stolen from her house? What if the holder of week five loses his job and cannot pay anymore? I began to ask people about their failed experiences with *tandas*, and they looked at me as though I could not possibly understand.

Which is true. Without formal language or notarized signatures; without "acts of God" clauses and any legal recourse; without the auspices of any institution, application, contract, or credit check; lacking any guarantee of payment and in the absence of interest payments—people seldom fail to pay. If the holder of week two loses her job after having drawn her full amount, *no pasa nada*—she will pay it back *poco a poco*. The glue that holds a *tanda* together is a community of people who have personal relationships with and trust one another. They have a connectedness, a *solidaridad*, that we who are worried about the shifting of responsibility for earthquakes and floods should envy. Unlike in our "sophisticated" financial systems, relationships are the collateral.

The shortcoming of the *tanda*, from a societal perspective, is that it does not encourage long-term saving or long-term thinking. Every day the small *tiendas* are filled with men, women, and children buying chips, cookies, Coca-Cola, and other items that are not only unhealthy but also expensive. These shortsighted spending decisions are the result of Mexicans' unfamiliarity with saving for the sake of saving, not to mention the marketing power of junk food manufacturers. And let's not forget the bureaucratic dysfunction, if not perceived corruption, of banks.

One week, Señor Roberto went to our local ATM to set some money free and came away 400 pesos short. He went into the bank at once to report the error. The bank manager assured him that as soon as the bank reconciled the day's ATM withdrawals, we would receive our money. After repeated visits and telephone calls (if, of course, the definition of a telephone call is that we call and they do not answer), the bank announced the reconciliation showed no discrepancies. In this country with corruption at every level, high and low, we suspected that someone in the bank was enjoying our 400 pesos. At the very least, we doubted the accuracy of the reconciliation. Everyone was very pleasant, *muchas gracias*, but no information would be forthcoming. There would be no recourse. *You can stop calling us now.*

Our US bank credited us the missing money, but for the working poor in Mexico, there is no remedy for the loss of 400 pesos, which could be a week's salary or more. It is a mistake most Mexicans cannot afford to make even once.

When Magali came to meet with us, we quizzed her on her reasons for wanting to buy a car.

"How will you use it if you cannot drive and the boys cannot drive?"

"José has a driver's license, and he can drive us." José was her brother.

"Where do you want to go in the car?"

She took time to consider this. "I want to take my kids to the hot springs outside town every couple of months."

This puzzled me. "Why not take a cab or the bus? It's less money than buying and maintaining a car."

"Because my cousin is selling his car cheap. He is desperate for the money. This would help him out."

We had arrived at the heart of the matter. The drive to assist a family member is very strong here, even if it means buying a car you cannot drive. And despite the fact that *tanda* participants are often poor by most economic measures, the *tanda* money can burn a hole in people's pockets. Short-term thinking drives impractical results—like deciding to buy a car because you have the six thousand pesos and your cousin needs them. The car? It is an incidental commodity in the transaction, a bauble, no more important than the package of cookies in the *tienda*.

Juan Pablo, who owns a car, gave Magali some information on the Care and Feeding of Cars, and she withdrew her application for the loan. She agreed that it would be better if José drove everyone to the hot springs in our car three or four times a year, a far more economical result.

Instead of a car, she bought a refrigerator and joined another *tanda* to buy a stove.

We Need Burros and Bricks

I EXHALED LOUDLY, like a whale that had been holding its breath underwater for a month.

"Chinese takeout?" I sputtered. The sun was setting on the second Sunday in May.

"Sure, why not?" Señor Roberto did not see the tragic implications of Chinese takeout on Mother's Day. He assured me that Jews eat Chinese takeout on many major holidays and nothing bad happens.

"Because Mother's Day, real Mother's Day," I said, "requires brunch with champagne and orange juice at an overpriced, crowded restaurant, my children solicitously surrounding me, their carefully chosen Hallmark cards extolling my considerable virtues; when everybody starts bickering about who insulted whom two Christmases ago, pass the champagne, please, and hold the orange juice, thank you very much. Followed by two aspirin and a nap."

How is it that after all these years of marriage he doesn't know this?

I was enjoying a "poor me" state of mind. I had

stepped off a curb and sprained my ankle on the mean cobblestone streets of San Miguel and was now relegated to a two-week stay in bed. So on Mother's Day, when Señor Roberto announced a craving for Chinese takeout, I felt underprivileged because it was Mother's Day, I was a mother, and I did not want Chinese takeout. If I had wanted Chinese takeout on Mother's Day, I whined, I would have moved to China.

Instead I had moved to Mexico, a place physically closer than China but psychologically far away from that familial champagne brunch. It is not as though I lived a Norman Rockwell life in which my children, my parents, my nearest and dearest were close by celebrating holidays with big, convivial dinners. The only Thanksgiving I ever had everyone together, including my ex-husband and his family, one dog peed on the rug from the excitement of the crowd and the other climbed onto the counter to eat the resting turkey. It was without doubt a two-aspirin-and-a-nap event.

But I miss my family, and when Mother's Day rolls around, I suffer from "life's not fair because on Mother's Day I regret living in Mexico, a place—oh, wait—where I *chose* to live" syndrome. This is the definition of a first-world whine.

And then, just when I was reaching the peak of my self-pity, an article in our local newspaper, the *Atención*, caught my attention. A young Mexican man, Rodrigo, had taken it upon himself to help an old couple who sold dirt for a living. He fed them when they came into San

Miguel, and sometimes they slept in his kitchen. He had begun to spread their story in the community to get help to improve their lives.

Let me introduce you. Doña Candelaria and Don Antonio Vertiz live outside San Miguel in a small settlement called La Campaña. They are sixty-five and sixty-seven years old, and they have sold dirt for their whole lives. They dig up topsoil, put it in bags, load it onto three mules, walk into town, and sell dirt door-to-door. What takes twenty-five minutes by car demands eight hours walking with donkeys. Those charming burros we see clomping down the cobblestone streets give harsh new meaning to the expression "dirt poor."

Doña Candelaria and Don Antonio sleep on the street until they sell the dirt, and then they walk the eight hours back. Stop here and think about this; don't just breeze by at eighty miles per hour. They are sixty-five and sixty-seven years old, and they spend one full day walking to town, two or three days walking across town to sell their dirt, and another day walking back. They lie on a sidewalk and have little food and no shelter. Okay, now we can go on.

For all this effort, like most of Mexico's extreme poor, Doña Candelaria and Don Antonio make less than US$50 a month. One of their sons died, leaving three children they are raising. They have no running water, not so much as an outhouse. Even in a poor country, their plight is desperate.

Rodrigo needed money to alleviate some of their

more pressing needs. I knew I could raise money with an e-mail to friends in the United States, but I wanted to see the situation for myself. There are thousands of stories here—stories of families who need doctors, disabled children who need medicine, people robbed and left homeless—and, as with everywhere, not all are true.

Rodrigo graciously took me to meet the family. We drove out of San Miguel and onto a dirt road, ending on a steep, rutted hillside that became impassable by car. Ten minutes of uphill walking on my now-healed ankle led us to the Vertiz "home"—a cave-like shelter of mud, rags, and cardboard, where they, aging adults and children, slept directly on the dirt floor.

There are at least eighty-two nongovernmental organizations in San Miguel helping individuals and animals in need, most staffed by both Mexican and foreign volunteers. Casita Linda, an organization that builds adobe houses for the poorest of the poor, is one. The day I visited the Vertiz site, the Casita Linda volunteers joined us to see whether they could help to build a small, one-room house. The San Miguel Rotary would raise money to buy bricks and concrete. The volunteers worried about walking the bricks up the hill to the land, since the truck could not make the last one hundred yards, but grandchildren and neighbors agreed to hand-carry each brick. This would be their contribution.

Rotary and Casita Linda covered the bases on building a shelter, so I went for the burros. All three of the Vertiz burros needed to retire. They were old, no longer able to reliably make the weekly trips into town. Time and inadequate saddles had worn down both fur and spirit, exposing bare patches on their hides and their souls. Of course, Doña Candelaria and Don Antonio couldn't afford new ones, and without the animals they could not make enough to live.

I hate to ask friends and family for money, but occasionally I am moved to do so. When I do, I have a mantra I repeat to myself.

"It's not about you," I chant. It never is. "It's not about what you want to do." I hate that part.

Then I fill in the circumstances of the case.

"Get out there and walk sixteen hours a week with three burros for US$12." I have to pause to let that sink in. "Then, after you've done that, if you want to, you can decide not to ask."

I asked.

People responded in the wonderfully generous way that marks us in the United States. The one-room house was built. The old animals were retired to green pastures; three younger burros and ergonomic saddles were purchased. In addition, there was enough money left over to buy bricks to rebuild the back wall of another outbuilding, providing a dry, secure sleeping place for the children.

Mexicans are not as familiar with charitable giving as Americans. Mexico ranks seventy-first out of 156 countries, while the United States consistently ranks in the top three. This does not mean Mexicans are not generous. They are. With large Mexican families and traditional communities, "charity begins at home," in the church and through social bonds like *padrinos*, godparents with the very real responsibility of stepping into the shoes of the parent when necessary.

I found out how important this bond is one day when I noticed our gardener's, Juan Pablo's, eyes were a watery red. "Ave María" was playing on the radio, but since "Ave María" plays every day I didn't think this was a cause for tears.

"*¿Qué tienes? ¿Qué pasó?*" I asked.

"My friend Balta was killed yesterday in a car accident, *señora*. Today is the funeral."

"Go, go," I said. "Go." When I hear these stories, I can guess alcohol played a part and the family left behind will now struggle for their lifetime and beyond.

Later I learned that yes, Balta had been drinking, fought with his wife, and drove off in his uninsured truck, which was totaled in the impact that killed him instantly. He was twenty-seven years old. Of course he had no life insurance. His twenty-two-year-old widow and his three orphans were now dependent on their Mexican community of relatives and friends.

I worried for his young wife. What could prepare her for such tragedy and hardship so young in life?

"What will happen to her?" I asked Juan Pablo.

"It is very hard, *señora*. She has no job, and she has three young children. She still has to pay for the truck, which is now worthless."

"What will happen to her?" No matter how many

times I asked, I knew there was no good answer.

"She will go live with her family, and her children are now my children."

"Your children?"

"Yes, I am the *padrino* of two of the children, so I must help them—money, food, school supplies, clothing, backpacks. It is a big responsibility." The generosity of the poor supports the poorer.

Helping people in poverty is complicated. In some ways, it is like hitting the broad side of a barn—no matter how poor your aim, immense need could be helped with a small amount of money. On the other hand, we must make personal choices about where we put our efforts. Doña Candelaria and Don Antonio have been digging topsoil on land they do not own for a lifetime, a practice that leads to environmental destruction. Should I say, "No, I cannot help them because what they are doing is environmentally unsound and illegal?" I don't know.

Some people help dogs, cats, and burros, while others insist, "The children are more important! They are the future." Some people work tirelessly for large organizations; others help as they can, one person at a time. In the end, we all make our choices, do what we can, and live with the ambiguity.

The other day, I looked at a photograph of Perla, one of the Vertiz grandchildren, a child with a laughing, sunny face.

Could you keep your smile in these circumstances? I asked myself. I knew I couldn't—I am the one complaining about Chinese food, complaining about Mother's Day, about a life that is not *quite* perfect.

We who have been blessed with extraordinary abundance should not congratulate ourselves on the giving of our time, money, or assistance. We should learn from those who find dignity and hope in hopeless situations, from the working poor who share what little they have with those who have less, and from the women like Balta's wife, Doña Candelaria, and millions more who commit their children to a harsh world.

I may not be willing to eat Chinese takeout on Mother's Day, but I am certainly going to stop complaining about it.

SECTION FOUR

CULTURE AND OTHER COMPLICATIONS

"The world in which you were born is just one model of reality. Other cultures are not failed attempts at being you; they are unique manifestations of the human spirit."
—WADE DAVIS

We Are Not the World?

————————

THE FIT OF EFFICIENCY taking place in my home office in San Miguel most closely resembled the weather phenomenon known as a whirlwind. To-do lists spun and swirled, and computer keys clicked out airplane reservations in July for a family Christmas. I reviewed and revised a rapid flow of long-term goals using multiple software applications opened on both a laptop and an iPad. A link to a *Time* magazine article, "The 10 Greatest Books of All Time," was loading up, and the wireless printer gasped and coughed out sheets of Very Important Papers. The forces of the universe aligned perfectly when a reminder popped up on my screen: time for a meeting with Señor Roberto to discuss the performance issues of one of the part-time workers at our home, Cinco Flores.

I laid out the problem.

"Maricruz is coming to work late, leaving early, and having problems in between. And Magali, our housekeeper, who is supposed to be supervising her, is saying nothing."

How is this possible? I see the same behavior she sees.

Yes, I am aware I am living in a foreign country, but hard work is the backbone of life everywhere, isn't it?

"We must speak to Maricruz very firmly," I said. "She needs to understand her work is not satisfactory." I tapped my pencil on my to-do list.

Señor Roberto nodded. I took that for agreement, so I continued.

"How will she get ahead if we don't tell her what she is doing wrong? Of course, be polite, but remember, if we have to fire her, we should not pay her any severance. We should be frank with her. That might motivate her."

Señor Roberto raised one eyebrow, perhaps at my use of the "royal 'we.'" Because of his more advanced Spanish skills, including the ability to speak in the past and future tenses, he was our go-to vocal technician. He would be the one to shepherd Maricruz onto the true and righteous path.

"Remember, severance is out of the question," I repeated. "Her work ethic is at fault here." I sat back and crossed the whole situation off my to-do list.

"I will discuss this with her," said Señor Roberto, "but I should talk to Martha first." Martha is our Mexican property manager. We rely on her for many things, but foremost among them has been navigating Mexican culture.

Three days later, Maricruz left us, severance in hand, having been assured that we loved her and her work but that we had no more money to pay her. It marked the beginning of the decline of my unchallenged, relentless efficiency, runaway focus on the future, and unbridled commitment to self-help—for others.

WHEN I CAME HERE, the idea that Mexican culture was different from US or Western culture did not occur to me. I did not hold the common stereotype that Mexicans are lazy. But I did think that I could see Mexico in the rearview mirror of the United States, maybe twenty or thirty years behind. *Someday*, I thought, *they will catch up, and then Mexicans will be like other North Americans.*

I knew for a scientific fact that we human beings are all the same, no matter our place of birth, our language, our color; we are born and we die, and more than 99.9 percent of our DNA is an exact match.

That is true but deceptive.

The real story is in the 0.1 percent difference. That is where the unconscious learned assumptions known as culture may play a starring role. Culture seems like something that could be easily identified and shed, like taking off a coat when the weather changes, leaving us naked, holding hands, swaying, and singing "We Are the World"—in English, of course.

To be sure, some cultural behavior can be influenced and changed. But social scientists are now finding that an amalgam of language, history, geography, climate, luck, and disaster—the stuff of culture—is much less like a layer of clothing and more like hardwired fact. While some genetic differences are involved, many scientists strongly suspect that most of these differences are cultural ones, meaning they arise from learning and growing up in particular places, in particular times, in particular circumstances.

We cannot always comprehend the immutable force of culture. It molds our minds and creates diverse ways of physically seeing, thinking about, and approaching the world. We are like fish that can never understand the role of water.

Those of us from Western, Educated, Industrial, Rich, and Democratic nations (i.e., WEIRD, so named by University of British Columbia social scientists Joe Henrich, Steven Heine, and Ara Norenzayan) see our own culture as superior, a banner leading others into the future. We are organized, we are planners, we are technologically advanced critical thinkers. But as it turns out, we WEIRDs are the outliers. Our fundamental thinking and perceptions are shared by only a small fraction of the world's population.

The reality is that within that tiny 0.1 percent gap, we live in vastly different realities.

OUR LAWYER, an older patrician gentleman, came to meet with us at our house one day. He entered the street door, and I watched him walk the long passageway, where he encountered Juan Pablo, our gardener.

"*¿Cómo está, señor?*" Señor Soto gave a slow half-nod as he spoke. "And how is your family? Good? Excellent! And things go well for you? *¡Qué bueno!*"

I wonder how he knows Juan Pablo.

Then he saw our housekeeper, Magali, and the same gestures, the bow, the effusive language, replayed. When he left, the scene unspooled in reverse, with endless iterations of *buenas tardes, que le vaya bien,* may your children do well, may your health be perfect. It was like a favorite, long-lost uncle had parachuted in for a brief but extravagant visit.

"How do you know Señor Soto?" I asked Magali. In this hierarchical society, I couldn't imagine him hanging out with a housekeeper and a gardener.

"I don't, *señora.* I have never before seen him." She looked puzzled I would even ask such a ridiculous question.

This language of respect shines a light on the Mexican cultural value of deference and personal dignity. Visible demonstrations of civility are required. Getting angry, being sarcastic, or insulting someone is counterproductive and guaranteed to be a problem in interpersonal relationships. Even gentle criticism delivered directly can be problematic.

Respect, expressed through politeness, is valued over all other personal characteristics. "You are a person of intelligence? Nice, but how are your manners?" "You are ethical? Good, but are you maintaining the social order of the group?" Initially, I found this to be unhealthy, inauthentic, not as honest as my own culture has taught me to be. But I have come to feel that an institutionalized code of etiquette, even if not heartfelt, can be therapeutic and valuable.

Go to a US website where a controversial topic is discussed, perhaps on race, Mexicans, women's rights, abortion, or guns. Read the comments. See what passes for civil discourse, and tell me if it's healthy.

Sometimes it is better not to know what people are thinking.

INSTEAD OF ADMIRING INDEPENDENCE, ambition, and the much-vaunted pulled-up bootstraps, Mexicans adhere first to family, then to extended family, and then to a community. Even the raising of children is communal, shared among aunts and uncles and *padrinos*. It is no wonder, then, that Mexicans often feel sorry for us, we expatriates, here alone without our families, whom we see only once or twice a year, instead of many times a day. Who supports us? What happens when the world crashes around us? Who picks us up when we fall?

The unconscious question for Mexicans is, "What do I need to do to serve these people who are my support?" The not-so-unconscious question for Western cultures is, "What is best for me?"

We were shopping in a small pottery store in a nearby town, and our conversation with the young clerk turned to the upcoming Mexican presidential election. He announced that he did not prefer the leading candidate but was voting for him anyway. Why? Because his uncle had asked him to.

"But," I asked, "how will he find out whom you voted for? Aren't the ballots secret in Mexico?"

Of course they are.

"Then couldn't you just vote as you wish and then say nothing, or just lie if he asked? No one would know."

His hand flew to his chest.

"No," he said, "he would not know. But, *señora*, I gave him my word. And he is my uncle."

MAGALI MARVELS AT MY focus on the future. That I can plan today to do something six months from now and then actually do it appears as *un milagro* to her and might indeed be a miracle in her life. In six months, children might get expelled from school, health problems could threaten, or family members might need help. Stability is fragile; it cannot be taken for granted.

Mexicans have had so little historical ability to influence their own lives that planning for the future seems a waste of time. If God is (or the gods are) responsible for what happens, then why plan? Human beings have no power anyway. I hear this in the language, in the passive voice, in the reflexive verbs. When something is broken, what I hear is *lo que pasa es que se rompió* ("what happened is it broke itself"). When we inquire about the future, "Will we see you tomorrow?" we often hear *si Dios quiere*—"if God wishes." Mexicans view the forces that cause things to break and those that determine what happens tomorrow as outside of them. They do not see themselves as being in control of their world.

If the universe cannot be controlled, why waste time

planning? Instead, Mexicans spend time relaxing, hanging out with family and friends—activities that have value, an investment in something that matters; it is not time wasted. Unless it's necessary, many do not want to trade time for money. And the future? The future is a repetition of the past—a cycle of events and traditions, pilgrimages, fiestas and saints' days, third birthdays and *quinceañeras.* The past is never past. It comes around again and again, posing as the future.

In sharp contrast, my e-mail inbox contains a blog post giving me "Nineteen Ways to Be More Productive" and a YouTube video called "We Are the Gods Now," since we will soon be transcending nature, if we haven't already.

CULTURES ARE ORGANIC SYSTEMS where there is no "better" or "worse." Some parts are good, and some are bad. By absorbing unconsciously what each generation before us learned, we free up our own brains to learn other things. The mistake we WEIRDs make is our unchallenged assumption that our culture and values are the ones the world aspires to—that others are coming along but lagging behind. Looking at culture requires a wide-angle lens and an open mind. When we bring the focus in too close, we see only small things—like plumbing.

I FLOPPED INTO AN EMPTY plastic seat at the airline gate in Houston with a sigh. The woman to my left looked up from the book she was reading and smiled. She was a woman of a certain age, wearing complicated makeup.

"Travel," she said. "It's a pain, isn't it? Where are you coming in from?"

"Mexico."

She frowned. Then she moved her suitcase away from me.

Misunderstanding, I said, "Oh, it's not in my way."

"No," she said. "It's not that. It's, um, I don't know how much you understand about Mexico, but, well, they are really dirty there." She glanced at me knowingly.

"Dirty?" I hung suspended like a trapeze artist in midair. Later, I delivered a soliloquy longer than Macbeth's about Mexican children who go to school spotless despite having no running water. But in that moment, I had nothing.

"Yes, you were there in one of the nice hotels, I can tell by looking at you, but . . ."

I opened my mouth to correct her, but she leaned in close over the endless loudspeakers shrieking departures and said, "Those people do not flush their toilet paper. It's a disgusting and dirty culture." She stressed "disgusting" with a snakelike hissing sound.

"Oh," I said, too aware that at Cinco Flores we do not flush our toilet paper, a consequence of not-quite-three-hundred-year-old city pipes.

"And so, of course, they have bedbugs." She shook her head side to side as she tsk-tsked.

"Bedbugs?" My voice rose two octaves.

"Yes, that's why I moved my suitcase. Bedbugs can jump from one suitcase to another." She smiled, happy to have enlightened me, a person with name-brand clothing and secretly unflushed toilet paper. She returned to her book.

After I got home, I cornered our housekeeper as she walked by my office.

"Have you ever had bedbugs?" I asked her.

"Oh, *sí*," she said. "*¡Qué horrible!* We had them once. A gringa came to our house and gave us used children's clothes, and we found out later that they were filled with bedbugs. We had to throw them out, and ours, too. Other than that, no." We stood together, shaking our heads.

"I am so sorry that happened." I wondered if the British were still apologizing for the diseases Captain Cook spread.

"*Ni modo, señora.* She was very kind to think of us."

Back in my office, I pondered these ironies. Given all of our technical mastery, why haven't we defeated bedbugs? Is it possible that We Aren't the Gods Now? That We Aren't the World? I picked up a book that was definitely not one of "the ten greatest books of all time" and curled up on my daybed.

Some days it may be better to lag behind.

THERE ARE RULES THAT STATE ...

———————

A LONG LINE OF PEOPLE and luggage wends its way toward the fluorescent-lit ticket counter in predawn León, Mexico, waiting to check in for the flight to Houston, now delayed by fog. These early-morning travelers twist, fidget, and crane their necks to see why the line stalls, why the American woman stands in front of the agent for an interminable time. I know. I am that woman, and I am attempting to travel with Lola the dog.

"*Señora*, you cannot travel with the dog. You must have the formal papers." The agent's olive-skinned, handsome face is as impassive as Lincoln on Mount Rushmore, his voice without affect. His posture reminds me of a saguaro cactus: straight, tall, and prickly. Before I can even present Lola's documents, he gazes over my head and gestures to the next person in line.

Lola and I stand firm. Another encounter with the Mexican bureaucracy has begun. I am experienced, having survived numerous Mexican bureaucratic battles, including:

- The Coordinated Assault on Remodeling a House in the Historic Center and the subsequent Siege to Register to Pay Taxes: a record nine trips to two agencies.

- The International Attack on the New Immigration Law (screenplay by Kafka), in which Señor Roberto did not have the correct legal documents to stay in Mexico but was forbidden to leave the country to get the correct ones in the United States, requiring double shuttle diplomacy between Inmigración at the airport and Inmigración in San Miguel. And the rejection of my visa application because I put a period after my middle initial, triggering a series of additional visits in which I always lacked just one key document that had not been mentioned the time before.

- And who could forget the National Health Insurance Registration Bivouac, where I had my blood pressure reading recorded: thirty seconds to take it; two locations, three visits, and five queues to write it in my file, by which time the 120/70 was a bit higher?

Here at the airport, I am a foot soldier in an army with few weapons, but I am not defenseless. I carry the only arms that will work for this dog-flying skirmish: a file folder of paperwork, the rules in two languages, up-to-date printouts of the weather, a measuring tape, an excess of courtesy, and a vocabulary of respect—as well as whatever patience has not already been killed by the Fortunes of Past Wars.

Mexico is so famously bureaucratic that former president Calderón sponsored a contest inviting his citizens to nominate the nation's most ridiculous and inefficient procedure. Competition was hot among the 20,000 entries, but the winner was a woman who spent between four and fifteen days a month traveling from office to office to get her son's lifesaving medication authorized: two doctors to authorize and four bureaucrats to stamp the application, all in different locations.

Mexico's extreme bureaucracy may be a legacy of the Spanish conquest—a living tableau of the verb *chingar*, to violate by force. Bureaucrats often use their power to *chingar*, to defeat others, to make others *el chingado*, the victim. It's a lot like kicking the dog. Today, I vow, that dog will not be Lola.

Back at the airport counter, we begin to tap-dance to the bureaucratic tune.

"*Señora*, the dog needs the formal papers from the veterinarian."

"But of course, *señor*." I put on my most cooperative smile and the singsongy voice required to talk to bureaucrats and almost anyone in Spanish. Respect is necessary if Lola is going to make it to New York.

From a file folder optimistically labeled "Lola Travel," I produce the official papers filled out and signed by the veterinarian, delivering them with a light but definitive tap on the counter. I show no fear and exude a slight whiff of authority. I do not want him to think I am a *chingada*. But not too much; too much can kill the whole thing.

He squints at the paper. He glances at Lola's airline-approved kennel.

"Señora, the *jaulita*, it is too big."

"Ah, *sí, señor*, it seems to be so, yes, I am able to see that, but *en realidad, señor*, I think the size is allowed. But let's measure it, as you may be right." I smile brightly.

"Agreeing while disagreeing" is a useful face-saving technique. If I say he is wrong, he will be forced to play his power card and Lola and I will be left at the airport like Tom Hanks in that movie. Agreeing while disagreeing buys time, a major asset in these encounters. As with water over rock, bureaucrats can be worn down.

I produce my red leather monogrammed tape measure in inches and centimeters from my purse. In accordance with the printed airline rules, it demonstrates that the kennel is well within the allowable size. The agent checks my numbers. The crowd shuffles and murmurs.

I am mystified. Whatever motivates his nit-picking the rules is not about the dog. What does he think is going to happen to a homeless dog who lived in the country without any shelter or food and who is on her way to the Upper West Side of Manhattan to live with my daughter, Jessica, who is, metaphorically speaking, the Sainted Virgin Mary, Mother of Dogs? Who has dog toys, for heaven's sake? And a concierge? The goal of the skirmish here is form, not substance. Similar to bureaucrats the world over, the agent gives not a whit for outcome, only for a fierce protection of his tiny part in the unwieldy exercise.

He attacks from a new angle.

"*Señora*, the dog cannot fly when the temperature is under twenty degrees anywhere on the route." He peers over my head to the waiting line.

I am prepared for this obstacle. New York can be frigid in December, but today the temperature is not below twenty degrees. I have a printout from Weather.com.

I move to the "What do you think?" strategy.

"*Señor, por favor*, would you do me the extremely kind favor of informing me what do you think is the temperature in New York today?"

He picks up the phone and dials out. After lengthy, rapid-fire Spanish, he informs me, "*Señora, desafortunadamente*, I do not know. The temperatures are in Fahrenheit, and I do not have knowledge of the conversion to centigrade."

I press my fingers hard to my forehead, as I realize he plans to keep my Lola from her forever home because of the temperature in New York, when he doesn't even know what the temperature *is* in New York. At this moment, other Mexicans, all too familiar with the game, become involved. The man next in line, seeing himself stuck until the end of time with Lola and me, steps up with his smartphone. He types in the temperature and holds it up with the conversion: 31 degrees in New York.

The stranger speaks to the agent in rapid, animated Spanish that I imagine is along the lines of, "For the love of all that is holy, sir, have you no mercy?" I sense a shift, a momentum, in my favor. I am within sight of New York City, if only I can get to the connecting flight in Houston.

But not yet.

"Unfortunately, *señora*, you need the special permission of the veterinarian to travel with the dog when it is below thirty-two degrees."

Here we have the final obstacle. I whip out the paper signed by the veterinarian allowing Lola to fly at colder temperatures. The corners of my lips twitch ever so slightly as I taste victory. The big file folder marked "Lola Travel" is now empty.

Sadly, sadly, but not really, the agent shakes his head while he studies the paper.

"But, *señora*, the paper lacks a stamp." He feigns regret and hands it back to me without meeting my eyes.

"Stamp?" My small smile becomes a growing grimace. Manhattan recedes into the far horizon.

"*Sí*, the stamp of the veterinarian."

"Stamp?" I thwack the counter with my fist, mimicking a stamp.

"*Sí, señora.* Without the stamp, how do I know the paper is not forged?"

THE MEXICAN BUREAUCRACY loves nothing more than a stamp, entire government offices thumping like dryers filled with tennis shoes as multiple documents and copies are imprinted. The number of bureaucrats and stamps that are required is in inverse proportion to the sheer impracticality and unworkability of the law.

In our local bilingual newspaper, a Mexican government official explains that a law (either new or previously unenforced—it is hard to tell) requires an import license to ship prescription medication into Mexico. This creates anxiety for many gringos with special medicines not available here or insurance that pays in the United States. I am interested because my gummy vitamins have been classified as prescription medication and can no longer be shipped to Mexico. All that I am, I owe to gummy vitamins, so I am concerned.

The official assures us that it is merely necessary to do a *trámite* each time the medicine ships. He utters this with great calm, but every time I hear the word *trámite*— i.e., going through a bureaucratic process—I see myself without food and water, stumbling through an overgrown jungle of a government office without a machete. Later, the official reveals that, oh, by the way, no one has *ever* been successful in obtaining the necessary permit. I am relieved. We will not waste our time on that strategy.

Our motto is "Nothing works, but everything works out." People are resourceful in disregarding and working around the law. Illegal ways of importing gummy vitamins will spring up, and I will join the majority of Mexicans, who disregard the law when necessary.

Mexicans, with a long legacy of unjust laws, believe that if a law is inequitable, obeying it is purely optional. In fact, studies done in 2008 asked Mexicans, "Do you think the people should obey laws even if they are unjust?" 71 percent said no. Who isn't convinced their taxes are too high and are used for the wrong things? An estimated 30 percent of Mexicans fail to report any income, and another 30 percent underreport. Who doesn't think electricity costs too much money? Ten million Mexicans steal electricity every year, either lacking the lines to hook up legitimately or believing the agency dispensing it is corrupt, or both.

All of this, of course, drives gringos crazy. We have a strong belief in the fairness of laws, carefully considered and consistently enforced. It is hard for us to understand that Mexican laws are not passed to be enforced consistently, if at all. They are aspirational. Four hundred eighty-nine amendments to the Mexican constitution have been enacted in the last one hundred years, during which time the United States has amended its constitution seventeen times, for a grand total of twenty-seven amendments. It's like having another pair of Jimmy Choo shoes with stiletto heels and pointed toes: they look fabulous, but walking in them is not a possibility.

In this relationship-based society, the laws are bent or broken, ignored or applied, depending on who you are and whom you know, and, yes, for money. The ability to get things done is often accomplished by bribery, or *la mordida*, "the bite." Everyday encounters between people, police, and local government are colored by "bites"—a regressive tax that plagues Mexico. I wonder as I stew at the ticket counter if that is what drives this intractable encounter. That at least would make some sense.

THE RISING SUN IS melting the fog. I have one last maneuver. I lick my now-dry lips and plunge in.

"*Señor*, I am so sorry I cause you so much trouble and take up your extremely valuable time. Why don't you permit me go to Houston, where the weather is sixty degrees?" I make a grand, sweeping backhand in the general direction of the United States to show how quickly I could be bounced to another bureaucrat.

"Then you don't need to decide if the veterinarian's letter is a forgery. Let those crazy gringos in Houston work it out when I try to go on to New York." This technique is popularly known as passing the buck.

In a flash, I am gone—Lola transported to cargo, and I escorted to the flight like the paper-forging, dog-exporting criminal I appear to be.

I worry that Lola and I will be living in Houston until the New York winter is over, but when I report to the airline counter to check in after passing customs, I notice the agent's name is Hernandez. I explain in Spanish that I live in Mexico and I am traveling with a rescued dog, who is going to live with my daughter.

"*¡Qué bueno!*" she says as she types in our continuing-flight information.

"I have a letter from the veterinarian letting Lola travel in temperatures below thirty-two degrees. It may be thirty-one degrees there today." I drop my bag on the counter to fish out the folder marked "Lola Travel."

"Don't bother." She looks up at me and smiles. "I'm sure it's fine."

A Conversational Fugue in Three Parts, No Harmony

A GENTLE BREEZE BLEW down from the mountains surrounding San Miguel. It picked up the murmur of the fountain on the patio, joined the voices of Señor Roberto and our friend Arturo, and carried their conversational fugue to my sunny second-floor window. We had enjoyed a midday meal together—mild poblano peppers charred and stuffed with creamy avocado and potato—while we discussed our renovation project. I like Arturo, but that short encounter stretched my Spanish to its limits. Even though I am proficient in laundry discussions, hours of Spanish conversation give me a headache.

The problem is thinking that *speaking* Spanish is *understanding* Spanish. No, like pitcher and catcher, Mexicans communicate in a code that goes beyond words. Octavio Paz observed that Mexicans live behind *la pantalla*, the mask, a result of years of conquerors, tyrannical governments, and a hierarchical caste system. In addition to simply refusing to share unpleasant information (like my gardener and housekeeper, who will not tell me about the plants with *plaga* or the broken hot-water heater), Mexicans use a number of nonresponsive and unusual linguistic work-arounds to limit risk, even when there is no risk. Here are the three most surreal, the ones that create maximum disequilibrium for the unsuspecting:

1. Do not be completely honest with anyone who has more power than you;

2. Do not offer information that is not specifically asked for; and/or

3. Use a lot of effusive language.

These patterns of conversation generate stress. So, when lunch was over, I pled work obligations and departed for my office, where I could overhear the conversation but not take part. In English, this strategy is sometimes referred to as eavesdropping.

"Does your daughter, María, have a *novio?*" Señor Roberto asked Arturo. Now began the *sobremesa*, the charming Mexican custom of chatting after a meal that can go on for as long as digestion itself.

"*Sí*," said Arturo, "she has had a boyfriend for the last six years."

Señor Roberto knows the obvious—Mexican families are large, complex, and important. When a conversational lull occurs, the topic of family can be mined like a vein of gold. It is the organizing principle of Mexican society for many reasons, including sheer numbers. At our gardener Juan Pablo's wife's brother's wedding, the mother of the bride, also known as Juan Pablo's wife's brother's new mother-in-law, informed us that she was one of eight children. Her husband, she told us, had seven brothers and sisters, and together they had nine children. In her most recent estimates, taking into account those she had that day inherited, she counted over one thousand relatives. She pressed me to imagine how wonderful that was. I tried, I did, but I couldn't. All I could think of was refereeing harmony at Christmas dinner.

I had to let go of the one thousand–person Christmas dinner to keep current with the conversation on the *novio*.

"*Sí*, he is a very nice young man from a good family."

I wondered. In my nonscientific analysis entitled Survey of Questions I Ask the Cook, with its corresponding and even less rigorous Inventory of Answers That Leave Me Wondering, I find that information in front of the Mexican mask is elastic and subject to change. This often requires asking the same question three times with an increasing level of precision to nail down an answer that conforms to reality.

ONE DAY I ASKED OUR COOK, Luis Fernando, if he could drive us to the bus station in Querétaro, a nearby city. I started with a simple question as we stood together in the kitchen.

"Luis, do you know how to get to the bus station in Querétaro?"

"*Sí, señora*, I can drive you. *Por supuesto.*"

Experience has left me not so easily fooled. "I can drive you" means, "Yes, I have a driver's license and I can operate a vehicle." I kept a sharp focus on the real question—did he know how to get there?

In the second round, I tried to lasso him back from his prior linguistic left turn.

"So, you know how to get there precisely?"

"*¡Sí, sí, señora!*" This was uttered in a tone similar to "What are you thinking? I practically live at the bus station." He squared his shoulders and his chest swelled.

Amateurs may end here, but they will not make it to the station in time for the bus.

Sí, sí may be translated by the optimistic as an enthusiastic "Yes, yes!" but in my Inventory of Answers that Leave Me Wondering, it often means, "Well, not exactly." This can cause confusion and an encounter with the surreal, not to mention unexpected changes in travel plans.

Now we came to the third round, requiring a deep level of specificity, where finally my training as a lawyer had a practical application. I asked, as though conducting a deposition, "Do you know how to get to the bus station, including how to get off the highway, get to the street it is on, and drive to the front door?"

"Oh, no, *señora*, I have never been there, so I do not know where it is."

Good information to have before we get started. Because we cannot get to the bus station in Querétaro if we have no idea where it is. Sometimes we cannot get there even when we do.

I WAS JOLTED BACK to the present when Señor Roberto went for another round on Arturo's daughter and her boyfriend.

"So, you are acquainted with his family?"

"*Sí, sí*," Arturo said, but a slight, almost imperceptible hesitation and his failure to add more information planted a seed of doubt. Remember, *sí, sí* may not mean "yes." Brevity can also be suspicious. In my survey, I often received responses delivered with a unique Mexican approach called Do Not Volunteer Anything Not Specifically Asked.

SEÑOR ROBERTO AND I were passing a small *farmacia* when I remembered I needed arnica, an anti-inflammatory pomade.

"*Señora*, I want to buy arnica, *por favor*." The clerk stood at attention behind the counter, looking very efficient in a white lab jacket.

"Ah, *sí*, but no, *señora*, there is no arnica here."

I was startled. I was positive I had purchased it there before. In fact, I believe every *farmacia* in Mexico carries arnica. A *farmacia* without arnica is like a *tienda* without Coca-Cola: highly unlikely.

"No arnica?" I faltered. Had I forgotten where I'd

bought it? Were they out? If I came back tomorrow, would they have it? How could I say any of that?

"No, *señora*. There is no arnica." She smiled politely.

"No arnica?" My mind began to search my vocabulary like a cell phone looking for a signal.

"No arnica." Her smile was fading with every repetition.

It didn't take a bilingual visionary to see the future of this conversation was a dead end. I tried a different tack.

"Did you used to sell arnica?" This was difficult for me in Spanish, as it required a verb in the past tense. I said something resembling "Do you have arnica but in the past?" A wild swipe of my thumb pointing back over my shoulder signaled the international symbol for a former time. At least I hoped it did.

"No." She looked sympathetic but moved away to tidy a shelf of shampoos. My allotted arnica-asking time had ended.

Puzzled, I inched toward the door. On their billboard with their specials, I saw *ÁRNICA CON ALOE*.

Relieved that my mind was still intact, I called out, "*Señora?*" She turned, and I pointed to the board.

"Look, it is written here." The question mark hung above my head.

"*Sí, señora*, that is arnica *con* aloe. You asked for . . . arnica."

I blinked. I stopped. I bought arnica *con* aloe and added another entry to my Inventory of Answers That Leave Me Wondering.

As we walked away, I asked Señor Roberto, "Do you understand what just happened?"

"Not a clue."

Learning to work with this system requires a high level of precision. If I call the swimming pool to find out if they are open, they may say yes, but when I arrive, there may be no water in the pool. I will be understandably frustrated, but, of course, I asked if they were open and, yes, of course, they were. The next week, I may call again and wisely ask, "Are you open and do you have water in the pool?" They may say, "*Sí, sí*, I am very happy to advise you, my esteemed client, that there is water in the pool," but when I arrive there might be only a paltry puddle of water lying there. When I call the third time and ask, "Are you open, is there water, and is there enough water to swim?" I will have achieved enlightenment, nirvana, and a half-dozen other altered states of being, and the answer will finally be "no."

SOMETIMES THE UNWILLINGNESS to tell bad news to anyone with more power than you collides with the language of respect as they hit the concrete wall of reality. This causes unusual meltdowns in front of your eyes.

Señor Roberto and I went to the *vivero* one day to buy plants. It was hot and I didn't want to load them into the car, so I asked *la señorita* if they delivered.

"*Por supuesto, señora.* What time should we bring them to you?"

This takes more words in Spanish than in English. In contrast with answers that are measured out with an eyedropper, Mexicans also pepper their language with elaborate conversational flourishes and archaic diction that we English speakers, with our directness, cannot hope to reproduce.

One winter, Señor Roberto sent a quick e-mail to our lawyer asking him a question. He ended it by saying, "Happy New Year." The response had a one-sentence answer to the question and an entire paragraph of wishes for us: may we have 365 days of health, happiness, good humor, prosperity, many grandchildren, and seven other improbable events while he respectfully awaited the favor of our forthcoming questions.

La señorita waited for my response on the delivery of my plants.

"No hurry. *No hay prisa*," I said. "But if I know what time you will come, I will have the money ready." They wouldn't carry change.

"But, *señora*, of course. At whatever time is convenient for you, *señora*." She bowed her head to show the deep respect she felt for me and my plants.

"No, *señorita*, please, what is convenient for you, your business, your deliverymen?" I asked. I almost continued, "for your mother, your father, your cousins . . ." but, as a friend of mine says, that would have been too much *crema* on the taco. The problem with the language of respect is that it is contagious and it can spread through your speech like invasive clover if you are not careful.

"*Señora, por favor*, it is my pleasure to serve you and to make the delivery at whatever time works for you and your family."

The top of my head started to melt, and my sunscreen expired. Señor Roberto frowned and sat on a large planter under a palm tree.

She waited, her pencil suspended above her pad to record my every wish.

"*Bueno*, then how about eleven o'clock tomorrow morning?"

Her smiling face transformed into a scowl in front of my eyes. She pursed her lips and exhaled with a loud whoosh of aggravation. She shook her head vigorously.

"But no, *señora*! We cannot do this! No, no, there is absolutely no way to do this! This is impossible! We only make deliveries in the afternoon!"

As we walked away, I said what I always say to Señor Roberto.

"Do you understand what just happened?"

He replied, as always, "Not a clue."

SEÑOR ROBERTO CIRCLED AROUND the *novio*-and-the-daughter story for the third time.

"So, is the *novio* a nice guy, steady, worthy of your daughter?"

"No, he has many problems; he is very troubled."

A long silence signaled Señor Roberto's entry into a dissociative state. Talking to Mexicans sometimes resembles eating hard candies with a chewy center. One has to keep assaulting the surface before getting to the surprise in the middle. Having now bitten down, Señor Roberto's teeth appeared stuck. But what choice was there but to go forward?

"What . . . kinds . . . of . . . problems?"

"Well, his mother, Guadalupe, made a lawsuit against her sister, Dolores, over an inheritance, and when Dolores won the lawsuit, Dolores's son was shot by two hit men that maybe his own mother, Guadalupe, hired. The two hit men failed to kill Dolores's son, but then two men shot and murdered his mother, Guadalupe, and now he, the *novio*, might be a suspect. But it might have been the same hit men his mother, Guadalupe, hired to kill Dolores's son, because she refused to pay them since they didn't kill him."

Here, he stopped to take a breath.

Needless to say, this family discord would come as a surprise in English, but in Spanish, there was always the possibility that I, a mere eavesdropper, had heard it wrong. Did he say *matar*, meaning "killed," or *nadar*, which means "swim"? Did the *novio*'s mother, Guadalupe, swim with her sister and the son who is the *novio* called the police because the sister inherited a poor ability to swim from her father? For me, listening to Spanish is like watching *Wheel of Fortune*—so many blank spaces and I need to buy a vowel. I didn't think Dolores and Guadalupe were swimming, but by this time my mind was.

It sounded like Señor Roberto did not trust his

understanding of the story, either. He moved to a technique we call the Spanish Synonym Game, where we try to derive meaning by throwing a flock of synonyms at the conversation and see if any will fly.

"You said *estaba asesinado*? You mean, like, 'she was murdered with a gun'?"

"*Sí*, like, murdered with a gun."

"And the son of the sister was *casi matado* but did not die?" "Almost killed" was as close as Señor Roberto came in Spanish to "attempted murder."

"Almost dead, yes, but no, did not die."

"And the *novio* of your daughter is a suspect, *¿sí o no?*" We often ask a primary question with the follow-up question "*¿sí o no?*" Since Mexicans frequently speak in a style that can be described only as "zigzag," the answer may be too long and complicated for us to understand. This suggestion that there are just two possibilities sometimes works. But not always. Today, Señor Roberto was lucky.

"*Sí, es posible.*"

I sighed, feeling dizzy. The lawyer in me wondered if it *is* necessary to pay a hit man who hasn't performed under the contract, but I did not wander there. Instead, I was grateful I was not in charge of refereeing harmony at their Christmas dinner.

SER, ESTAR, AND THE CHARMS
OF LIVING IN SPANISH

MY HOUSEKEEPER, MAGALI, arrived for the day to find me wrapped in a blanket, slumped on the sofa. A sniffling, stuffy-nosed, leaky-eyed cold had made my head feel as solid as a basketball.

"What's wrong, *señora?*"

"I am *triste*," I said. "I am sad because I cannot breathe."

"*¿Triste?*" She blinked and frowned.

"*Sí, triste*," I repeated, this time more loudly. Did she not know the word *triste* in Spanish? How was that possible? She was the one who had taught it to me when I cried for days over the death of a dear friend.

"She was too young to die!" I had wept for her motherless babies, her rudderless husband.

"*Muy triste, señora, muy, muy triste.*" Mexicans know more than anyone that no one is too young to die, and so we moved on. But *triste* stayed in my vocabulary, along with the sadness.

Apparently on this day, instead of saying I was *triste* because I could not breathe (*respirar*), I said I was sad because I could not vacuum (*aspirar*). Magali's look was a cross between confusion ("*¿Qué pasa?* She hasn't vacuum-ed since she has lived here.") and a general acceptance of things that cannot be understood when you work for *los gringos*. ("*¿Quién sabe?*")

Similarly, Señor Roberto once told our lawyer (our *abogado*) he was grateful to have him as our avocado. If I had been the listener, I would have been rolling on the floor laughing. Instead, our lawyer smiled as though he appreciated being held in the same general esteem as guacamole.

This scenario repeats itself in ways too many to mention as I travel the long, unpaved road to living in Spanish. Since the route is filled with potholes, I often ask myself, *Why bother?* Plenty of people live in Mexico without speaking Spanish. *I don't have time to do this*, I tell myself. *I am too old*, I whine. *I will never, ever be fluent.* That at least rings true.

But I have kept on, propelled mostly by guilt. What I lack in aptitude, I try to overcome with persistence. That endears me to Mexicans, who are not like the French, who are said to be contemptuous of anything less than an expert attempt to communicate. No, Mexicans will smile like delighted grandparents, clapping, cooing, and astonished at the progress you have made in butchering their language. Mexicans are also known for their willingness to make gentle corrections to hapless Spanish speakers' attempts. There is a story about a bus robber who is moving up the aisle, taking money from the passengers. When he gets to the front, a gringa announces, in slow and deliberate Spanish, "*No tiene dinero.*" The robber carefully removes her wad of money, ineffectively hidden in her décolletage, and politely advises her, "No, *señora*, do not say '*no tiene.*' The correct form of the verb is '*no tengo.*'"

It is not all dark clouds. Cognates can make life in Spanish easier. What is a cognate? It is a word in Spanish close enough to its English equivalent to make you a danger to society. For example, "hospital" and "actor" are the same as their Spanish counterparts. Others, like *creativo* and *problema*, add a vowel on the end of the English look-alike. Some, like *probablemente*, use a slightly different ending. Many non-Spanish-speaking North Americans create their own cognates, announcing confidently that a "trucko" filled with "gravelo" will soon be delivered. Oh! I do not recommend this method of speaking Spanish, but what it lacks in accuracy, it makes up for in reduced study time.

Now, armed with these cognates, hit the streets. Enter a restaurant with friends and observe rambunctious youngsters from the United States running wild without parental supervision. Watch a male friend comment to the server that our countrymen's children are ill behaved and he is *embarazada.* The Mexican waiter's eyes will jolt wide open as though he has swallowed the *muy picante* habanero sauce, because your friend has chosen this special moment to announce that he is pregnant. Surprise! There are false cognates, too. This makes living in Spanish risky.

Another fun thing about Spanish are the endearing upside-down punctuation marks. These little creatures are there to help us understand whether the sentence we are about to read is asking ¿, exclaiming ¡, or both ¿¡, which is my personal favorite. I find that I am often questioning and exclaiming in the same breath (¿!*What the hell* ?!).

But mostly, Spanish is too challenging. Whose idea was it to make the word for straight ahead (*derecho*) almost the same as the one for going to the right (*derecha*)? Do we even know the number of gringos who are permanently lost as a result of this word warp?

I also strenuously object to putting the direct and indirect objects before the verb. Instead of saying, "Give it to her," as I would in English, first I have to think: Are "it" and "her" indirect or direct objects? Then I have to convert to Spanish; but wait—if that happens to be *le lo*, I have to change it to *se lo*. All of this transpires before I arrive at the action. By this time, the person who was going to "give it to her" has called an ambulance because she thinks I've fallen into a deep coma. But I am not in a real coma; I am receiving a message that my brain's hard drive, where I store the lyrics to the songs of the sixties, has maxed out.

Griselda, my Spanish teacher, announced one day that we would be learning the imperative, or command, verb forms. Unfortunately, Spanish verb tenses seem more numerous than fruit flies. I was still trying to learn the past tenses. I was not ready.

"I have never even heard of this." I scowled, as though this whole thing were Griselda's fault, instead of the fault of the entire Spanish language.

"Because no one in your household speaks to you in the command form, it is for you to speak to them."

Even if I could learn it, which was doubtful, I knew I would not be speaking to my housekeeper in the imperative ("bring my dinner"; "do the laundry"; "clean the house"), because even when tempered with the ever-present *por favor*, it sounds too staccato, like popcorn clattering around a hot pan. To avoid giving offense, I fill my Spanish with ways to say things in the longest, most indirect way possible. I say, *"Señorita, por favor,* is it possible you could wipe this terribly dusty sink today if it is not too much trouble and if you have the time?" Maybe the hacienda *patronas* are using the imperative with their housekeepers, but I am not. I expect this tense, too, shall pass.

Griselda has also tried to persuade me to use the familiar (*tú*) form of the verb. It's too hard, I told her, to figure out whom you are familiar with and whom you are not. It raised so many existential questions for me, I decided long ago to be on formal terms with everyone.

"At least," pleaded Griselda in a final push for sanity, "use the familiar form with your husband, Señor Roberto."

No, I told her. I don't think so. First, a little formality

in marriage is not a bad thing, and second, why learn a whole new ending for just one person?

Just as a symphony is more than the sum of its notes, Spanish, a high-context language, cannot be understood by its words alone. Meaning is both obscured and augmented, as is the idiom of music, by tone, pitch, and pace. When I ask the plumber, "Will you be here tomorrow, *señor?*" and he replies, "*Sí, señora,*" I can translate *sí* as "yes," but can I make out the texture, the timbre, the arrangement of sound and silence? Probably not. Living in Spanish, I need to listen, not only to the lyrics but also to the interconnected relationships of the world around me and the speaker and then hope and wait. Hope he will come tomorrow; wait until he does—two concepts that are, conveniently enough, expressed by the same verb, *esperar.* Which, by the way, sounds like *respirar* and *aspirar* and will, without doubt, get me into more trouble than a squeaky violin at Carnegie Hall.

Señor Roberto isn't bothered by this as much as I am. He employs an easygoing style that doesn't lose sleep over whether the subject and verb are parallel, or if his feminine articles are gliding along hand in hand with feminine nouns. He charges smartly through the underbrush, swinging a big machete, and everyone understands. I am tiptoeing through with a scalpel and people are asking me if I want to vacuum. When I ask him what verb tense he used, he tells me either the past improbable or the future unlikely.

Señor Roberto is also earning a degree in street

Spanish, also known as swearing Mexican-style, a robust art form in which an alarming volume of colorful, vulgar phrases are hurled and twirled around at the speed of a particle accelerator. Although I understand that swearing in Spanish is considered by some to be the ultimate sign of language mastery, I have a hard time conquering *pinche puto pendejo baboso*. It has too many words that begin with *p* and a meaning that fluctuates like the tide. It can mean almost anything bad, but can also be used, like most Mexican swear words, to greet your best friend. Don't ask me to give a translation—suffice it to say you will not want to use it with your mother.

The payoff in learning Spanish is to be able to take a peek into the mind of a culture so different from ours, a place where to give birth is to "give to light" (*dar a luz*), where *maleducado* means not that a person is without knowledge of algebra or physics, but that he does not conform to the extensive stylized rules of *cortesía*, like greeting people with *buenos días*, calling them *señor* or *señora*, or knowing what to say when you pass between two people on a narrow sidewalk (*¡Con permiso!*).

It is a place where just *being* is so important that there are two verbs, *ser* and *estar*, to choose from. To express being happy as a mental state in Spanish, I have to make a fundamental decision about whether happiness is permanent, a part of my essence. If it is, I use *ser*. If it isn't, because it is temporary and tomorrow I may be unhappy, I use *estar*. Making this small distinction makes me a different person.

There is a lot to love about this language. I am another person in Spanish, someone with no name but a title, La Señora, saying less because I can't say more, forced into a simpler existence because I am always on the frontier of what I can understand.

I love the gentle way it requires us to focus our attention on certain very different perspectives about life. In Spanish class, I once used the temporary verb *estar* to indicate, "María is my friend," and the permanent verb *ser* to say, "Jose is dead." A lifetime of living in English tells me friendship is temporary: friend me on Facebook today, block me tomorrow. And as for death—well, what could be more permanent?

Perhaps, but not here. Here, living in Spanish, friendship is permanent and death is temporary. That changes everything.

PROTECTION AGAINST COLDS AND FLU

A RECENT FEBRUARY MORNING finds me at a small sunny table at a café on a corner of the Jardín. I have my coffee, an opportunity for people-watching, and the *Atención*, our local weekly bilingual newspaper. I love the *Atención* because it provides useful information dished up with a dash of unintentional humor. It has a sensibility, even in English, that is as surreal as Mexico itself.

I am always happy that it is published on Friday, because, although the old routines of school and work are now seen only in the rearview mirror of my mind, they are, as the mirror says, closer than they appear. Friday still seems like a day to take a few minutes to relax, look forward to the weekend, and celebrate having (mostly) slain the weekly dragons.

I dive into my newspaper. Under the headline "Protection Against Colds and Flu," I expect to find an announcement of a clinic doing mass immunizations. It catches my attention because I need to get a flu shot here in Mexico, since I didn't get one when I was in the United States at Christmas.

But instead of the flu shot, I am invited to come to the front of the parish church, where I will be given the blessing of San Blas, the patron saint of throats. Blaise (Blas in Spanish) was a doctor who, while walking to prison, saved a child who was choking on a fish bone.

My mind is open to this offer of alternative medicine. I have had many flu shots that were ineffective against the flu, so why not try San Blas? But the final paragraph gives me pause. I am told that San Blas was martyred by a beheading in 316 AD. I reread this last part. Beheaded? Like he had his throat cut? Is someone with that kind of luck with his own throat the right person for the job? Is this a joke? But no, it is Mexico.

I am used to deep irony and strange encounters. In fact, I am sitting here because of a surreal, ongoing battle that has caused Señor Roberto and me to be voluntarily evacuated from our house on Friday mornings.

It all started with an innocent-sounding telephone call. The caller identified himself as an employee of one of the local banks and asked for "Xóchitl."

I said, "*Desafortunadamente*, you have the wrong number." When he called back within ten minutes, I felt I needed to elaborate.

"No, Xóchitl doesn't live here or work here; in fact, I do not even know anyone named Xóchitl, and if I did I would not be able to say her name because that *X* in the beginning is a real problem for me." (The *X* is pronounced like an *S*, so once you get the hang of it, it is not too hard. *Xóchitl* is like "So Chill." At least, that is the way

I think of her.) *Desafortunadamente*, no one seemed to care that Xóchitl was not here, because a few minutes later, the employee of the bank called again.

I got Magali involved, thinking that the caller did not understand my Spanish. Which was probably true but not relevant.

Magali told him the same thing using more words. Nothing deterred him.

"Why are they calling us every Friday, asking for Xóchitl?" I asked. "Do they only get to the *X*'s at the end of the week?"

"*Probablemente, señora*, she owes them money and they are trying to find her." Magali has some personal experience with this problem.

"But she isn't here, so how will they find her? How will repeated calls to a place where she isn't help to find her?"

There is no answer to these questions. This is the meaning of surreal—two realities: actually finding Xóchitl and just asking for Xóchitl. There is a surfeit of surreal here: I once read a story of a man whose death was declared a suicide by the police. *Okay*, I thought. But the article went on to mention that he was shot three times. Needless to say, I spend a lot of time rereading here in Mexico.

I worried that my new imaginary friend, Xóchitl, was in trouble. Perhaps evil men had kidnapped her aged grandmother, she had taken a loan to pay the ransom, and now she had lost her job and could not pay it back. *Focus!*

I told myself. *We just need to stop the endless phone calls that have become like the infamous Chinese water torture. Xóchitl will have to fight her own battles.*

Eventually, Señor Roberto spoke to someone at the bank with more authority than the person getting a fingertip callus from hitting redial.

"You must stop calling us." Señor Roberto told the manager. "There is no one living or working here named Xóchitl."

The manager told us that, of course, he understood our aggravation, and, yes, it must be extremely irritating to get a phone call every ten minutes for several hours asking for the same person who did not happen to be a member of our household. But, of course, surely we could see that the burden was on us to prove that we were not Xóchitl. We would merely have to bring proof that our telephone was registered in our names.

This was easy in theory but difficult in practice. Señor Roberto tried many times to prove that we were not Xóchitl, but often the manager was not there and no one else could help. Or there was just one more paper that needed to be notarized by someone who didn't really exist and therefore, like the bank manager, was extremely hard to find. I wanted to suggest that the manager just look at us to see that neither of us was Xóchitl, but I knew that would not work.

What to do? After gnashing of teeth, and fits of trying to curse in Spanish ("Is it *pendejo puto pinche baboso?*" I asked Magali. "No, *señora*," she said, smiling, "it is *pinche puto pendejo baboso*"), Señor Roberto suggested that we simply leave the house on Friday mornings so the phone would ring to no answer. He would run errands and I could sit at the Jardín and read the newspaper from cover to cover.

Maybe Xóchitl would appear at the bank and settle her debts. Maybe Señor Roberto would drop by the bank and the manager, the correct documents, and a non-existent notary would all be there at the same time.

But that all seemed unlikely. More likely was that eventually they would forget about Xóchitl. I planned to enjoy my Friday mornings with the newspaper and do the same.

THE RHYTHM OF RELIGION

THE JARDÍN, THE HEART CENTER of San Miguel de Allende, buzzes like electric wires humming a B-note. Women with babies, old people with Spider-Man and Tinker Bell backpacks, a gnarled man hunched into the shape of a question mark with too-big flopping shoes and a worn feed sack stuffed with clothes and tied with rope—everyone carries something. On a converted 1979 Volkswagen bus, the Virgin's image flashes, resembling the neon sign of a honky-tonk bar. I am drawn to the massive wooden doors of the church, where latecomers gather twenty deep, murmuring Mass like mourning doves. Inside, the benches overflow, spilling people into the aisles. The acrid trail of copal and wood smoke mingle in the outside air. My watch reads 5:00 a.m.

It could be just any fiesta day in San Miguel—the birthday of San Antonio; a day for the blessing of dogs, seeds, or taxicabs; the anniversary of the radio station—but it is not. It is the kickoff of the annual pilgrimage to the small church of San Juan de los Lagos, more than one hundred miles away. The *peregrinos*, the pilgrims, face nine days of walking punctuated by raw January nights. Mexican religious devotion, a tapestry of poverty and faith, of the sacred and profane, of modern and ancient, is being played out in surreal Technicolor. Suddenly, everyone drops to the ground, chanting. I drop, too, and pray for their safety and their—well, who knows what to pray for when you have been oppressed for almost five hundred years? From where I sit, God either isn't listening or has given up.

I admire their devotion. At the same time, I question the decision to be gone from work for nine days, often with no pay, sometimes with no option to return—to leave a business abandoned. What drives this? In my worldview, nine days of salary could buy something useful. But then I, a gringa to the core, with steady income, old enough to retire but still working, am in for only a half-day of walking, a fundraising effort for the prevention of domestic violence. I need to be back by noon for a conference call.

A Mexican friend helps me out. Here, she says, where a majority of the people are resource-poor, pilgrimages are often the repayment of a debt to an image—in this case, a fifteen-inch statue of the Virgin made of painted and varnished sugarcane paste that resides in San Juan de los Lagos. Here, where many people live outside the arms of a safety net, the Virgin, the saints, and their many images are as much an asset as a bank or a medical clinic. They are the benevolent family members people turn to for help with their big problems. If my child needs surgery, I do not put my faith in doctors. I pray to an image of the Virgin to cure her, and in doing so I create a *manda*, a promise. I repay my holy line of credit, the generosity of the Virgin's attention, by walking to her church annually, sometimes for many years to come. If I cannot walk, I bring food to the pilgrims, the poor feeding the poor. I take my unwritten *manda* more seriously than any contract drafted by a lawyer, more than any loan or charge-card payment. The Virgin must be repaid. If I do not have a problem requiring help, *¡qué bueno!* I walk to thank the Virgin for that blessing. I walk because everyone walks. It is a communal event, creating a rhythm to the days, months, and years of Mexican life. If it's January, it's time to visit the Virgin in San Juan de los Lagos. Next year we walk again, the future a repetition of the past.

Brilliant klieg lights in the predawn dark put the scene in sharp relief. A drum-and-bugle corps competes with a troupe of indigenous dancers as the Volkswagen I dub the Virgin Mobile begins to inch through the crowd. Like most things Mexican, the scene is eclectic, hallucinogenic, and anything but somber. We wait our turn to enter the long line of *peregrinos* as it bends away from the square.

I tuck my hands into the sanctuary of my armpits for a jolt of warmth as I look at the people around me, a band of ragtag walkers. Young men and boys lug handmade crosses of crude wood, some as tall as they are, decorated with religious images and nailed-on photographs of family members. Others carry huge, framed Virgin icons strapped to their backs. Old women wear skirts, sweaters, and dresses over pants, their entire wardrobe seemingly walking with them.

I turn to speak to a young woman carrying a baby in a cross-body rebozo. With her long hair parted in the middle and covered with a shawl, she looks as if she could have emerged from a Raphael painting of the Madonna.

"*¿Camina todos los días?*" I ask. I wonder how she will walk with the child for nine days.

"*Sí, señora,*" she says, "we go all the way to La Virgen."

"Does someone walk with you?" She smiles shyly at me and gestures around her.

"*Mi familia, señora, mi madre y padre, mis hermanas y hermanos, treinta por todo.*"

CHRIST AND CROWN, cross and sword—Hernán Cortés arrived with a Spanish agenda. Catholicism came with Cortés, but it was made Mexican by the Virgin of Guadalupe. In 1531, the story goes, as the Franciscans began the forced conversions of *los indígenas*, the Virgin appeared to Juan Diego, a poor indigenous man. Virgin images have popped up in many places over time (a car wash in New Jersey, an underpass in Chicago), but this virgin was radical for her time—she was brown-skinned and spoke Náhuatl, the language of the Aztecs. The roses she gave Juan Diego to take to the local bishop stained her image on his cloak, and within seven years, 8 million indigenous people were converted. For better and for worse, the marriage between old world and new was forged.

The indigenous people were warriors themselves. They had conquered and been conquered. When they were conquered by Cortez, they knew the price of losing and the value of adaptation. They took on Catholicism, but on their own terms. They accepted those parts of the religion that made sense to them but kept their old traditions: idolizing many images; using music and dance for festive, communal religious days. Mexico may have the world's second-largest Catholic population, but it is unique in its eclecticism, its vibrant inclusion of *los indígenas'* ways, its expansive view of what is holy. Catholic missionaries themselves encouraged many of the old traditions, like the local deities and the endless fiestas, to "sweeten" the conversion process.

There are many Virgin images here, but the Virgin of Guadalupe is the undisputed mother of Mexico, the ultimate contradiction in a country of contradictions. She is an indigenous representation of a white European religion, a Catholic with the symbols of nature decorating her cloak. She has united *indígenas* with Spaniards, *indígenas* with *indígenas*, and galvanized Mexicans inside and outside Mexico for almost 500 years. She led Hidalgo into the war for independence in 1810 and marched with César Chávez on the road to Sacramento in 1966. Today, she inspires both the devout and the secular, her image adorning everything from garage doors to cowboy boots. She represents the underdog, the oppressed, the feminine.

It is not important to believe her ancient narrative. It is enough to know that, more than the accuracy of her story, she is the image of the Mexican people. Octavio Paz observed that after centuries of failure, Mexicans believe in only two things: *la lotería* and La Virgen.

IT'S APRIL, two weeks before Easter and another opportunity to walk with pilgrims, this time with an image of Christ known as Nuestro Señor de La Columna. The narrow street leading to the main square in Atotonilco is jammed with stalls selling steaming corn tortillas and pungent fried pork, huge clay pots of *frijoles*, religious paraphernalia, cheap jewelry, and votive candles. It is eleven o'clock at night. If I didn't know it was a religious procession, I would guess Carnival.

My cab driver shrugs and indicates he can't move any farther through the crowd.

"*¿Puede caminar?*" he asks.

I get out. I am about to walk for six hours. What's another hundred yards?

I join the masses of devout Mexicans who will walk to San Miguel, many with canes, some carrying babies, others pushing wheelchairs and baby strollers on this arduous overnight journey. They accompany El Señor, a statue of Christ that is reputed to have halted an epidemic almost 200 years ago. The silent cavalcade begins at midnight and enters San Miguel at 6:00 a.m.—six hours to walk seven miles. I calculate that if I ran, I could cover the whole distance in seventy-seven minutes. But the biers that carry the shrouded images of Christ, Mary, and John are heavy and there are many stops—time for reflection, time to share the burden.

It's not about how fast we go, I remind myself as the crowd begins to shuffle en masse from the square; *it's about the journey*. Still, I have to slow myself down to keep faith with the lumbering pace.

As it turns out, many people cannot walk that slowly, and we leave the biers behind us. My flashlight battery fails five minutes in, so I glide along, disconcertingly disconnected from the ground. Two hours later, as I rise to the top of a small hill, I see a mirage-like scene: a field drowning in light, looking like a refugee camp with food vendors. People lying in the dry grass bundled in Snow White blankets and worn cotton bedspreads rest with their families and wait for Christ to catch up for a 3:00 a.m. Mass. I lie down, too, wondering how it is possible that it is so frigid in April when we have ninety-degree temperatures during the day. I don't get out much at 2:00 a.m.

I curl around myself to conserve body heat, the parched smell of dry earth waiting for rain swirling around me. I wonder why these people who work so hard, many who worked all day today, will walk overnight, sleep in a cold, dusty field, and wait for a statue.

The answer is complicated. *Los indígenas'* personal

devotion to sacred images still echoes through Mexico today—images regarded as beloved family members, alive, real, breathing. Their communal lifestyle is part tradition, economic necessity, and an affirmation that you are not alone—sorrow and joy are better when shared. Religion reverberates with firecrackers, magic, and contradictions, the past as indelible as a tattoo.

I take off my shoes and rub more blood into my frozen toes, my back against a wire fence. I refocus my eyes to see what I can see. The field is just a field. Nuestro Señor de La Columna is as lifeless as the column he leans on. Vendors hawk simple home-cooked food: tacos wrapped in plain paper, lukewarm coffee in Styrofoam cups. The sacred seems absent. But if I look with different eyes, I can see the faint outline of a different reality: people who mark the rhythm of time with their saints, icons, and families; people whose devotion and self-sacrifice sanctify a barren field with their hope; people for whom the threads of sacred and profane are so tightly woven there is no way to tell where one begins and the other ends. They are walking forward, looking backward.

Maybe they are prisoners of history. Maybe it's a waste of a night's sleep. Who's to say?

IN 1968, 96 percent of Mexicans identified as Catholic, women bore an average of seven children, and Catholicism was a growth business. Today, a fertility rate of 2.2 announces that times have changed. While Catholicism brings solace to an often poor, uneducated population, for some it has failed. Today, only about 83 percent of Mexicans identify as Catholic, and a swell of other religious groups, mostly Evangelicals, has made inroads into the Catholic monopoly.

I ask Magali about an upcoming religious holiday. "I don't know, *señora*. I am not a Catholic anymore."

This surprises me. I don't think I have met a Mexican who is not Catholic. "Really?" I hesitate. I lack the vocabulary necessary to discuss religious pluralism in Spanish, but I turn down the radio so I can hear her.

"No, I am a *cristiana*." This is the Spanish word for the new Evangelical groups springing up.

"What is the difference between being Catholic and being a *cristiana*?"

"If you are *católica*, you go to church and you repeat chants and you perform *rituales*. The *rituales* bring people comfort, but I don't want comfort anymore. In my new church, people help us understand how we need to live, why we need to stop drinking, why we shouldn't have babies when we are sixteen just because our mothers did. Now I ask God to help me make a better life."

I look at her, one of seventeen children, nine of whom died in childhood, her mother an alcoholic, her father unknown, her childhood one of unspeakable poverty. A better life doesn't seem like too much to ask.

Despite the still-large percentage of the population identifying as Catholic, no state religion exists here. Mexico began to disentangle religion from the state in

1833, secularizing education, taking Church lands, giving legal recognition only to civil marriage, and precluding the Church from having any national political role.

Now, despite the views of either the Church or the newcomer Evangelicals, modern Mexico has begun to legalize abortion, birth control, and same-sex marriage.

Yet visual reminders of religion remain everywhere. In churches, of course, but Jesus statues stand among the Coca-Cola and chips in small *tiendas*, an altar presides over the bus station. I give a wide berth to any shrine of the Virgin of Guadalupe to avoid being hit by reverent taxi drivers who bow and cross themselves as they drift onto the wrong side of the road. Mexico may be modernizing, but within her vast borders, many hearts stay rooted in the past.

MUSIC BLARES WITH THE thumping boom of a Latin beat on this already-hot Saturday morning in the Jardín directly in front of the parroquia, the main parish church. Here the contrast between ancient and modern Mexico is set in boldface—young women in tight workout clothes scream their approval when César, our Zumba leader, turns his back to us and bumps and grinds, his hips moving with the fluidity of well-oiled ball bearings. At the same time, tiny, stooped women in tattered dresses with shawls on their heads weave through the crowd and up the stairs to the church for Mass. Bells call the faithful while loud Latin music calls the adherents of the religion of Zumba. But even the girls in tights cross themselves as they arrive.

Later, in Los Angeles, I come upon a church message board that proclaims SUNDAY—JESUS SAVES! MONDAY—WE HAVE ZUMBA. The rhythm of religion is exquisitely complicated the world over.

I can't help wondering what happens on Tuesday.

How I Learned to Love Fiestas

THE MULTICOLORED BALLOONS bobbed happily on loamy-smelling gusts of wind that would soon bring rain. Metal folding tables on the dirt floor of the patio were wrapped in thin, opaque plastic sheets anchored at the sides with clothespins. Bottles of tequila and Squirt graced each of the eight large tables. Ominous dark clouds matched my mood. The one thing worse than enduring an outdoor fiesta is enduring it in the rain.

As soon as we made our way to our seats, Señor Roberto leaned over and asked, sotto voce, "How long do we have to stay?" He needn't have whispered. We were the only ones speaking English at Natalie's third-birthday party. As frequent invitees to family fiestas, we always puzzle over the question, "When can we leave without appearing ungrateful?" Mexicans have an endurance, a stamina, for fiestas that makes the Ironman triathlon look like a game of shuffleboard at a senior center. Heaven knows, we puny old gringos cannot last that long.

"At least until the birthday girl appears."

I could have added, "And I hope it is soon." We were

actors in a play where we did not know the script. Señor Roberto had developed his own strategies for survival, but not me. I hated fiestas. At the same time, I felt guilty that with all I love of the culture, I did not appreciate this very Mexican art form.

From birth to death, Mexican family life is a rhythm of rituals marked by fiestas. Marriages, certainly, but also birthdays like this—in this case the third, an opportunity to present the child to the Church for a special blessing. In the not-so-distant past, if children lived to be three they had a good chance of surviving to adulthood—something worth celebrating. The *padrinos*, the godparents, take care of the necessary arrangements in the church, buy the satin ball gown or white suit the three-year-old wears, and contribute to parts of the festivities. They can also be called upon to support the child if bad things happen to the parents. An even more elaborate fiesta opportunity is the young girl's fifteenth birthday, the *quinceañera*, a rite of passage into adulthood complete with the requisite ball gown, a posse of young friends, and a strangely choreographed *vals*, or waltz, reminiscent of a surreal French court dance imported into a dusty Mexican village.

Señor Roberto inclined his head to my ear.

"Let's stay until after the food."

The chicken leg and homemade mole with rice and beans would be made and served by the women in the family, some contributing the chicken, others the mole, beans, and rice. It would come on a Styrofoam plate with a plastic spoon, and I would again make a mental note to slip a metal fork into my purse for the next fiesta. Chicken legs and plastic spoons are like oil and water—they do not mix well. Mole is not easy to remove from clothes.

"Yes, after the food." I did not glance at him or whisper. Instead I smiled, nodding my head and looking around as if I were saying, "Isn't this the most fabulous thing you can imagine!" instead of repeating the instructions for our escape.

I leaned over to tell Señor Roberto something, but he was gone. I saw him up with the two hired musicians, ready to launch into the only song he knows in Spanish, "Camino de Guanajuato."

"*No vale nada la vida. La vida no vale nada.*"

Señor Roberto yodeled "*na . . . da . . .*" for many long, painful seconds to underscore the lyrics' major point—life is worthless.

"*Comienza siempre llorando, y así llorando se acaba . . .*"

"It always begins and ends with crying" is not particularly rollicking, and it doesn't seem like the appropriate jumping-off point for celebrating a three-year-old's birthday party. But mariachi music is standard fiesta fare.

Mariachi music is part of the cultural identity of Mexico. Ranchera, or "country," music is commonly performed by seven or eight musicians playing violins, trumpets, and guitars, dressed in the traditional tight pants and short jackets adorned with silver. Mariachi groups are usually men, but there are renowned Mexican female mariachis as well. The incomparable Lola Beltrán began her career as a mariachi singer with the Mariachi Vargas. And, unlike in other types of singing groups, there is usually no lead singer. They take turns.

For the less wealthy, two guys in blue jeans will do. Mariachi music focuses on love, betrayal, death, politics, and heroes. It snowballed in popularity after the 1917 revolution when the Mexican government began to try to forge a new cultural identity. New technology—in this case, the radio—then spread this once-regional music out across the new country's vast spaces. The lyrics and tunes are simple and straightforward, but they have an intense emotional impact.

One May night in San Miguel, at the height of the 2009 swine flu pandemic, when Mexico was virtually on lockdown, we ate at a local restaurant. We rarely eat out, but we had developed a program of solidarity with the struggling restaurateurs, whose places stood empty and forlorn while US tourists stayed at home, too frightened to come to a place with no reported cases of flu.

Two musicians entered with their guitars and their usual question: "*¿Música, señor?*" Usually we decline, but that night in May we felt so sad, so pained at the economic suffering around us, that we agreed.

"Do you play 'Camino de Guanajuato'?" That is like asking if the pope is Catholic.

"*No vale nada la vida . . . La vida no vale nada . . .*" Like Mexicans everywhere, we sang along and we wept. The waiters, the cook, and two gringos—together we sang for love and loss and for things we did not even understand. Mexicans love to sing along with mariachis, an exuberant practice often fueled by the tequila with which both fiestas and mariachi music are closely associated. The greatest mariachi composer of all time, the man who wrote "Camino," José Alfredo Jiménez, died at forty-seven from cirrhosis of the liver.

Tequila contributed to my own fear of fiestas. When we were invited to our plumber's daughter's *quinceañera*, I worried about the normal rules of social engagement—what time to appear, what to bring as a gift, what to wear, how to communicate with my impossibly defective Spanish. I had a cold, the weather was raw, and the fiesta was outside. It was impossible for our plumber to tell us what time to arrive, but he finally he decided on three o'clock. At four o'clock, the many women in the family were still cooking the food, and the fifteen-year-old *festejada* (having ridden back from Mass in the back of a pickup truck) wore a tattered parka over her floor-length satin dress, which dragged over the raked dirt of the yard. Every empty table had a bottle of tequila and a bottle of Squirt standing guard in the center.

I was a fiesta novice. No margaritas? No wine? No Diet Coke? ¡No problema! I was not going to start drinking Squirt at this point in my life, so I went with tequila. Straight. The first unusual thing I noticed was that I was speaking fluent Spanish with our contractor and I was warm for the first time in days. Hours, many hours later, I remembered having watched the strangest tableau—a very nervous fifteen-year-old, boys in formal clothes, girls in color-matched dresses, a very stilted dance routine—and then the next thing I remembered was having woken up in my bed. Since I did not recall how I'd gotten there, I felt sure something unfortunate had happened.

"I had this surreal hallucination," I said to Señor Roberto the next day as I described my memory of the dance scene. "It must have been the tequila."

"No," he said. "That is what it actually looked like."

I was, of course, not the first to fall, literally and figuratively, to devil tequila. The Aztecs had a myth starring Mayahuel, the goddess of pulque, the intoxicating drink made from maguey, and Patecatl, the god of healing, who had a one-night stand and then produced 400 offspring—all drunken rabbits. Comparatively speaking, my encounter with tequila was not so horrible.

Especially in poor families and villages, the rituals of the fiesta are very costly. Even simple homemade food for a hundred people represents a large expenditure. Add to that the tequila, tables and chairs, a band, and occasionally a stage worthy of Central Park. I thought of these expenditures as foolish and irresponsible. I wasn't alone. Even as far back at the 1700s, upper-class Mexicans clucked over how much money the poor spent on their fiestas.

How do they afford it? Our plumber tells us everyone in the large families chips in. One is in charge of the stage, another the band or the tables, each according to his or her ability, a familial redistribution of wealth.

Families borrow, save, and do extra work to fund these special events. But more to the point, as Octavio Paz observed, "Fiestas are our only luxury. They replace, and are perhaps better than, the theater and vacations, Anglo-Saxon weekends and cocktail parties, the bourgeois reception, the Mediterranean café." They are communal, not individual, extravagances.

By the time Juan Pablo's daughter Carla's confirmation fiesta rolled around, I had survived *quinceañeras*, third birthdays, and graduations from *secundaria*. I teetered on the verge of post-traumatic fiesta disorder. Like a person with no imagination, I wondered the same thing every time we were invited: *Why us? Can you not see we are awkward, we sit like wallflowers? That we try but we cannot understand how to fit in? Could I send a gift and not come?*

Never mind. I could not bear to decline the invitations, to hurt feelings, to suggest we were lacking in gratitude for our adopted culture.

For Carla's confirmation, in addition to a gift for the confirmation girl, I decided to take smaller gifts for the many children who are always there. After pondering what I could get for everyone that would be both readily available and enough fun to cover the span of their ages, I decided on colored pencils, crayons, and a pack of index cards. The fiesta was not in full swing when we arrived (we were two hours late), so I kept my little treasures in my purse.

Soon the clown who was entertaining the children with balloon animals began to entertain the adults.

Clowns frighten me, so I went inside the house to see if I could help with the food. When I returned from the kitchen, I was shocked at the scene. Señor Roberto had been pressed into service by the clown and was using a two-foot-long oblong balloon to mime urination in a corner. Mexicans love risqué humor. The adults howled and doubled up in laughter. The children gathered to see what was so funny. Even though I did not understand the rules of fiestas, I felt that swinging a two-foot-long pretend penis at a children's birthday party was potentially more explosive than singing an off-key version of "Camino de Guanajuato." I grabbed my purse and began jumping up and down, dangling my colored pencils like puppy treats.

The children flocked to me. I took out my stack of index cards.

"Let's write our names on the cards," I suggested in a high, semi-hysterical voice, "and then we can draw a picture and we will have"—*What?* I thought wildly. *What will we have?*—"a name tag!"

Soon, Señor Roberto was released from his part in the bawdy play and I had so many aspiring artists that I took over a long table to accommodate everyone who wanted my attention.

Shy Edgar tapped my arm and pointed out his name, nicely done with a backward *E* and a bird perched above the upward branch of the *d*.

"*Muy bien,*" I cooed to his sweet round face. "*Bien hecho.*"

Simple colored pencils and crayons are materials these children do not often have in their homes. Natalie brought out other art supplies I had given her the year before. Soon the index cards had handmade holes punched with the point of a paring knife and were tied around slender necks with garden string. Children careened around the tables, driving Big Wheels with their name tags flying behind them like arrows in the wind. The fiesta passed in a flash while I was engaged as a preschool art teacher.

I love these children. They are easy to please and their rules are clear: *See me! Like me!* Their Spanish is better than mine, but the gap is smaller. They have made me a connoisseur of the tools of my trade. I have scissors, a paper punch, ribbon, pipe cleaners, glue, and paint. When I go to the States, I am always looking for the unusual—things like glitter glue and colored tape. My art box stands ready to go to a fiesta at a moment's notice.

Now, after Señor Roberto has sung "Camino de Guanajuato," I get busy on craft projects. I have spoken strongly to Señor Roberto about not getting involved with clowns, and I have promised to never again touch tequila. When he says, "How long do we have to stay?" I reply, "Until the children get tired."

Given that they are Mexican and fiestas are in their genetic makeup, that could be a while.

THE ENVELOPES ARE MADE WITH LOVE
BUT HAVE NO GLUE

MIDMORNING, THE MEXICAN SUN was on its way from hot to hotter. I lay sprawled on the shaded sofa, coffee on the armrest, computer in my lap. The air smelled as fresh as sun-dried cotton. Señor Roberto sat in a more upright posture, also holding a mug and a computer. The weekly high-technology ritual known as the reading of Sunday papers was under way.

"Hey," I said, "here's a woman who has an MBA and she's marrying a guy who is a clown." I am big on the democratization of America as seen through the lens of *The New York Times*'s wedding announcements.

His eyes glanced up from the editorial page. "Is he a real clown or a politician?"

Señor Roberto was not the wedding wonk and follower of the *New York Times* Vows section that I was. I daydreamed of having our daughter's wedding mentioned in the *Times*, where the simple, formulaic language of each announcement was a guilty pleasure—a peek through a small window into one of the most loving days in the life of a family.

But then the daughter got married and I discovered the map is not the territory. After the hardening and tempering called wedding planning, after 110 paper-flower napkin rings, 12 cactus centerpieces, 24 organza table covers with hand-frayed edges, and more, I developed my own hand-frayed edge. I knew if I were the reporter writing the wedding announcement for *The New York Times*, I would be communicating with more reality, more edge, more like this:

> *Mr. and Mrs. Robert K. Merchasin are not entirely happy to announce the engagement of their daughter, Jessica Jordan Phillips, to Robert Forrest Rieske, not because they don't like Robert Forrest Rieske—they do—but because they live in Mexico and they are very busy and the bride is thirty-three years old.*

Just a year earlier, upon receiving the news of their engagement, I had jumped up from my computer and run into Señor Roberto's office. I was happy for them, but I had a major issue.

"Does this mean we have to plan a wedding?" I asked. "*I am very busy,*" I announced in a thin, whiny voice, "*I am in Mexico, and a mother whose daughter is thirty-three—well, what are* my *obligations?*"

While I was hoping I didn't have any, I received a call from Jessica.

"Why don't we get married in San Miguel?"

A wedding in Mexico! So many beautiful and interesting possibilities—fireworks, giant papier-mâché puppets, mariachis, and a flower-bedecked donkey carrying jugs of tequila through the cobblestone streets! My vast experience with Mexican fiestas could finally be put to good use.

At once I went from a disinterested mother of the bride to one with color-coordinated work folders and a mission/vision statement: everything would be done in Mexico and be handmade. I began to use exclamation points—a punctuation mark I hate! This would be my own Mexican fiesta!

Mr. and Mrs. Robert K. Merchasin are trying to cordially invite you to the wedding of their daughter, Jessica Jordan Phillips, but we request you understand that we are in a foreign country and just the process of getting invitations printed has made us question the feasibility of the entire event.

In line with my mission/vision statement, I ignored advice to have the invitations done in the United States. Instead I chose Sergio, an engraving master working as his father had before him, using a 150-year-old printing press. I picked the thick, creamy paper to be hand-embossed. I took his picture posed with his machine.

"Are you sure about this?" Señor Roberto said, rubbing the space between his eyes with his thumbs as if he had a headache.

I said, "What could go wrong?"

Here's one thing: envelopes are not available. Never mind, Sergio told us—he would make them by hand. I was nervous, but we were well into the invitation process, so I pressed forward despite a suppressed undercurrent of anxiety. The day everything was finished, I read everything backward and forward. I exhaled. I was smug.

"Ha!" I said to Señor Roberto. "Everything is perfect."

In the middle of the night, I woke with a delayed realization: the envelopes had flaps, but the flaps had no glue. How is it possible to make both the outer and the reply envelopes with no glue? Is it that nothing here is mailed? Did I need to have asked for the glue separately? In Mexico, envelopes can be sealed with stickers, but the US Postal Service, Beverly Hills branch, from where the invitations were to be mailed, does not approve of stickers. Its regulations also do not approve of items that are too thick, don't bend, and, maybe, are nonstandard custom envelopes made by Sergio.

Señor Roberto went to Los Angeles to visit his family carrying the glue-less envelopes—a man on a mission for envelope glue, a product sold online exclusively by Betty, who actually happened to live near LA. I stayed in San Miguel, concerned that I was mailing the invitations in the United States, a country where the federal postal service probably could not be bribed.

After a Sunday trip to Betty and other insurmountable obstacles requiring the exporting of envelopes across international borders, state lines, and a fair amount of aspirin, the invitations were mailed—thanks to the groom's loving family, who administered psychotherapy to Señor Roberto while applying glue with hair dryers.

Try to remember, I told myself between tantric deep breathing exercises, *it's only a wedding.*

The bride-to-be conducted a one-woman parade of wedding dresses that looked like they had come from the costume department of Gone with the Wind *while the mother of the bride cried.*

The bride-to-be, also known as my daughter, Jessica, invited me to join her and the maid of honor in New York City for the monumental task of choosing a wedding dress. The women involved in a wedding have titles like the bride-to-be (hereinafter the B2B), the mother of the bride (the MOB), and the maid of honor (the MOH). In general, men are not referred to by their titles, except for the father of the bride (the FOB, please, not the SOB), as in, "Will the FOB now please step forward with his checkbook?"

Before I left for New York City, I had lunch with a friend whose daughter had married two years before in an extravaganza resembling the chariot scene in *Ben Hur*. I mentioned the upcoming wedding-dress excursion.

"Take Kleenex," she said.

"The price?" As I was then deeply involved in wedding budgeting, it was my only guess.

"No, silly. It will just bring you to tears when you see

her in the first gown. That is when you will realize she is all grown up." She emitted a small sob just remembering.

I didn't mention that it would be cheaper to hire a psychiatrist to help me grapple with that reality than to buy a wedding dress. No, I heeded her advice. Armed with ample Kleenex and my credit card, the three of us invaded the wedding-dress store, where the dressing rooms were hazy with perfume and female anxiety. Bending under armfuls of bead- and embroidery-encrusted silk, frothy chiffon, and fluttery taffeta, the B2B and the MOH headed for the dressing room, where the MOH assisted the B2B into dresses that were either two sizes too small or three sizes too big. When she emerged in the first one, I took one look and reached for the Kleenex.

"Mom, why are you crying?"

I blew into my Kleenex and went for the truth.

"Oy," I said, resorting to Yiddish, as I often did to express deep feelings of dismay, "because I wouldn't get married if I had to wear that dress." Luckily, she agreed.

Time and endless dresses passed, and from under the ruffles, flounces, bustles, and trains, a simple, elegant dress and a happy B2B, MOH, and MOB emerged onto the streets of Manhattan, poorer but with Kleenex to spare.

The mother of the bride wore a pink, one-shouldered, ruched frock, which was selected by committee and in which, it was noted, she looked fat.

I was going to Chicago for work a few months after the bride's dress was safely purchased. I was looking forward to a visit to Nordstrom to buy a MOB dress. A week before the trip I sprained my ankle, so I had to resort to Plan B.

"What are you doing?" Señor Roberto asked as I lay in bed and pored over pages of dresses printed out from the Nordstrom website.

"I am buying seventeen dresses for the wedding." I typed my credit card number, now memorized, into the blank space.

"That seems excessive, even for you."

"No, I have a strategy. I am buying seventeen dresses online that might work, having them sent to my hotel in Chicago, and trying them on without walking to the store. Then I'll return the ones I don't want."

"Oy."

As it turned out, I eliminated twelve dresses but could not decide on The One, so I carried five back to Mexico with me. The B2B had requested I have pictures taken, so I brought them back to San Miguel, put a camera in the hands of the cook, and did a little fashion show for the housekeeper and the gardener. When they clapped, cooed, and exclaimed over the dresses, I forgot that most Mexicans won't say anything to *la patrona* that she doesn't want to hear.

The B2B is not Mexican, however, and her comments were instructive.

"That dress makes you look like Wyatt Earp before

the whole O.K. Corral episode," she e-mailed.

When I looked at the picture, I could see what she meant. On another work trip, I expanded my search to Saks Fifth Avenue and another four dresses. Dresses came. Dresses went. I skulked through airports like the dress smuggler I was. I canvassed friends, neighbors, and total strangers for their opinions. Two days before the wedding, a decision was made, which, in keeping with all decisions made by committee, was unsatisfactory.

Later, when we got the wedding pictures back, I said to Señor Roberto, "Why didn't you tell me I looked fat in that dress?"

He rubbed his left temple as if he had had a one-year headache and sighed.

The flower girls wore matching white dresses and carried orange organza and ribbon-adorned baskets spray-painted white, all made by the mother of the bride, who showed distinct signs of an unhealthy fixation on a mission/vision statement.

"Do you even want flower girls?" I asked Jessica. The 110 handmade paper-flower napkin rings were starting to drag me down.

"Of course we do. The only drama in the ceremony is whether one of them will bolt."

Lacking young children, and in line with my mission/vision statement (done in Mexico, handmade), we invited the daughters of our gardener, Juan Pablo, to be flower girls. I searched for dresses, socks, and shoes. I made color-coordinated flower pins that required organza to be "sealed" by running the edge through an open flame while Señor Roberto checked our insurance for fire coverage. The acrid smell of burning organza lingered as I wielded two glue guns, attaching ribbon to the spray-painted baskets.

Our Mexican staff found all of this unusual. Mexican weddings, like most fiestas, are loving events, but, to our eyes, are often quite informal. The prior year, Juan Pablo had invited us to his wife's brother's wedding.

"His wife's brother's wedding?" I had said. "Do we even know him?"

When we arrived at the reception, there were 400 people sitting at tables in the place that yesterday had been the site of a corral holding many of the animals we were eating today. A living, flowing river of mud covered the floor of the enclosure, the result of recent rains. The women of the family served food, sliding perilously—ice skaters in stilettos. A year later, I asked Señor Roberto if he remembered the time we went to Juan Pablo's wife's brother's wedding. "How could I forget?" he said. "The mud is still in the car."

At Jessica's wedding, neither of the flower girls bolted, but Natalie, just three, balked. Carla, the oldest, sensing an end to her own fifteen minutes of fame, first gave her an encouraging push. On the second balk, Carla escalated to a full-scale shove. The congregants drew a simultaneous in-breath as they looked to see if there would be ripped dresses, scuffed shoes, blood, and piercing screams. From my front-row seat, I tottered back up the aisle in my skyscraper heels to rescue Natalie, who then walked quite nicely.

Nothing makes a wedding more memorable than a flower-girl debacle.

The couple was married by María de Lourdes Bravo Villanueva, an officer of Mexico's civil registry, a logistical feat rivaled only by Hannibal's crossing of the Alps with war elephants.

I was unswerving in my desire to have a Mexican legal ceremony because *The New York Times* will only cover a wedding if the legal ceremony is within six days of the celebration. In other words, the legal ceremony had to take place in Mexico. The B2B indulged me. The groom and Señor Roberto expressed little more than minor alarm. *The New York Times* had to be persuaded that the Hague Convention of 1954 recognized Mexican weddings as legal in the United States. After the fourth trip to the civil judge of San Miguel, everyone else wanted to swerve, but I held firm. "Remember *The New York Times*," I chanted. "Remember the mission/vision statement."

We were filled with stereotypes and assumptions about the intertwining of marriage and religion in this Catholic country, but our encounters with the civil judge blew them away like a hat in a March wind. No priest, rabbi, or minister can perform a legal union in Mexico. For that we needed María de Lourdes Bravo Villanueva. A ceremony in a church is only the optional icing on the wedding cake.

Then, whatever ideas we had about the roles of Mexican men and women were shattered by the aspirations expressed by the Federal Marriage Message, a document read at every civil union in Mexico. Because it inspired and surprised us, Señor Roberto made this translation: "Here lies the essence of the couple. You are making of yourselves a small engine which will energize the world around you through your actions, and through those of the children that you take the responsibility to invite into the world. You . . . face each other eye to eye; you are two equals, with no duties, rights, or obligations which apply only to one of you."

Yes, it is possible to learn a great deal about a country from a wedding.

The mother of the bride wore a valiant smile throughout the wedding, despite a seating chart mix-up involving papier-mâché Chihuahuas and the late-breaking news that there were no dessert plates for the cake.

Imagine that the MOB had a table of ten people identified by papier-mâché parrot heads on a big seating chart, but instead of parrots the artisan delivered Chihuahuas, since he was out of parrots, but the printing of the seating chart had already been done and identified ten people as parrots, not Chihuahuas. And that when the caterer informed the MOB that it was time to cut the cake but there were no dessert plates, she wanted to shout, "People, I am trying to do a wedding here!" but instead she sent someone to the store two blocks away for Styrofoam plates, the kind used on the street for tacos.

Imagine that when it was over, she gazed heavenward and whispered, "Thank God it was only a wedding."

Jessica Jordan Phillips married Robert Forrest Rieske in a celebration complete with fireworks, giant papier-mâché puppets, mariachis, and a flower-bedecked donkey, surrounded by the loving friends and family members who felt brave enough to leave the United States and come to Mexico. There were no fatalities, kidnappings, or beheadings. The only injuries were self-inflicted and tequila-related.

It was only a wedding, but it was wonderful. *The New York Times* wrote its own Phillips-Rieske wedding announcement for the Sunday paper, but I liked mine better.

SECTION FIVE

DEEPER INTO MEXICO

"Wherever you go,
there you are."

—ARISTOTLE, CONFUCIUS, AND BUCKAROO BANZAI

Some Things Make No Difference, or How La Señora Got Hot Water

---

IF ANYONE HAD ASKED ME back in that Mexican restaurant in Philadelphia, the one where we made the decision to move to Mexico, whether I thought I would become a different person in a foreign country, I would have said, "That's ridiculous—of course not." After all, I had moved five times in eight years across the United States, and I had always experienced exactly what Aristotle (and Confucius, Buckaroo Banzai, and others) said: "Wherever you go, there you are."

But secretly I hoped that I would find some other, better self in Mexico. Don't we all hope that something, like having more money or that gorgeous pair of shoes, will make us happier, better people? I do not need the current research on the brain science of happiness to know that money and shoes don't work. Mexico has proven it to me as surely as any scientific study.

After eight years in San Miguel, with all its charms,

challenges, and cultural complications, I had the opportunity to go deeper into Mexico, to experience an even more unfiltered life in a Mexican village. I found myself living part-time in a one-room casita at the best undiscovered beach spot with all its limitations—scarce grocery items, one restaurant, and Internet service so slow that whatever few bytes there were dropped from the wires in impatience and meandered arm in arm on the dirt roads.

And, for the first six months, no hot water.

The problem emerged after the construction of our casita when the water was turned on and trickled daintily into the kitchen sink. I could almost count the drops as they fell. I put my hand under the tiny stream.

What's with the water?

I don't remember my exact words, but probably I said, "What the hell?"

Señor Roberto explained. "There is no water pressure. That is why the water is only dripping. And without water pressure, the on-demand hot-water heater doesn't get triggered, so, in addition, the water is cold."

I was apoplectic. Could we have the world's worst plumbers? How was that possible?

Solutions were discussed. Raising the ceiling and redoing the pipes were rejected. A Canadian friend, a physicist turned plumber (I know that's unusual, but Mexico brings that out in people), made a house call. He inspected the plumbing. He shook his head sadly.

"Pump," he said. "Get an in-line Grundfos pump."

While I was still asking, "When can it get here?"

Señor Roberto focused on calling Home Depot, many kilometers away.

"*Sí, señor*," the very helpful salesman told him, "we can get this exact pump for you. You need to come in to order it and give a deposit, and we will call you when the time comes to pick it up."

Señor Roberto patiently explained that we lived *hundreds of kilometers* away from Home Depot. Was there no way we could order the pump and make the deposit with our credit card?

No and none.

Another person was called to the phone.

"*No, señor, no es posible en México.*"

With every new person, he described our great need for a Grundfos in-line pump and the *hundreds of kilometers* separating us from Home Depot. I could see the *hundreds of kilometers* flying by the car window as he spoke.

After grinding his way through four polite but unimaginative employees, Señor Roberto encountered Bernardo. Bernardo agreed on the impossibility of making the deposit with a credit card, but he revealed that we could do it with a bank transfer in the amount of the pump. Then, when the pump arrived, he would call us and we could drive there and get it.

Nine phone calls and one bank transfer later, we waited, one of us patiently and the other not so patiently, for the arrival of the pump. Every day I asked, "Did they call?"

"No. Not today."

We called them.

"Yes, *señor*, they came in, but you were not here and we could not hold it. They are all sold now."

Señor Roberto put the telephone down while Bernardo was still talking, removed his glasses, and tapped his bald head three times on the desk. Then he picked up the phone, put his glasses back on, and calmly pushed forward. It is necessary to be polite in Mexico, but a much-needed expression of frustration unknown to the other party is permitted.

"*Sí*, I understand, Señor Bernardo, but we have already paid. The money is right there in your Home Depot account. Can you not hold the pump when it is already paid? *¿Sí o no?*"

This was a foreign idea to Bernardo, dreamed up as it was by impatient people who equate time with money, are wed to efficiency, and do not want to spend an extra day driving to Home Depot and back.

No, he said, but perhaps the next shipment would be coming soon.

And indeed, the long-awaited day came when a Grundfos in-line pump with our name on it appeared at a Home Depot hundreds of kilometers away. Señor Roberto jumped into the car in the early-morning hours to go and retrieve it.

When the pump and the two plumbers arrived at our house, the suspenseful process of installation began. I was tense. I decided it was a momentous enough occasion that I would live-tweet it.

Pump installed. #beyondhappy
Pressure improved in shower. #getnakednow
No hot water. #Uh-oh
Water in bathroom runs only when water is on in kitchen.
#Whatthehell?

I described this to a friend, who asked me the same question that I had asked myself: "Why do you continue to work with these guys if you think they are the world's worst plumbers?"

Because we have become like most Mexicans: the relationship is more important than the plumbing; these men are wonderful people, and they need the work. One is pushing three sons out of poverty by sending them to university. The other lost his wife to cancer in April 2014. When he told us in July he would now be going away to be with his dying brother, I did not know the words in Spanish to be of any comfort. When he cried, I cried. I patted my heart with my open palm in the universal symbol for *I am thinking of you; I care about what happens.* And we cried harder.

Is this relationship not more important than plumbing? It would not have been in my former life. I would not have had the relationship to begin with.

THE OTHER DAY, when I thought about that Mexican restaurant in Philadelphia, I laughed. The Mexican restaurant I go to here is a *taquería*. A *taquería* serves only tacos and the occasional tostada and quesadilla; there is no guacamole, no salads, not even flan for dessert. A roll-down metal garage door secures a small room facing a simple town square. Scuffed plastic tables and chairs are assembled on the street. Styrofoam plates are covered with plastic bags so the plates can be reused. There is no kitchen; everything is cooked out front. No margaritas, just cervezas and soft drinks. I bring my own wine in a screw-top jelly jar. No mariachis, not even a boom box. It is not charming or elegantly rustic.

But the woman who runs it, Maricela, is my Spanish teacher. She taught school during the day for thirty years, and she and her family have run the *taquería* at night for the last twelve. She is a force of nature in this village—keeping children out of trouble, marshaling resources for a kindergarten swimming academy, watching out for the elderly who have no family (this last, a fate worse than death in Mexico).

Is this not more important than the menu, the mariachis, the margaritas?

My images of Mexico are an inventory of large and small acts of kindness and generosity: Magali, who wanted to borrow money to buy a car to help out a cousin; Juan Pablo sharing what he has with Balta's fatherless children; Rosa, who adopted a child left by a desperate Honduran mother; strangers on buses, in *tiendas*, on the street. Mexicans have modeled tremendous kindness and generosity for me. I want to go back to the woman who complained about Mexico and toilet paper at that airport gate in Houston and say what I could not think to say then: Are plumbing constraints more important than the spirit of openheartedness that flows here? The Buddhists say that generosity is the virtue that produces peace. Could we not all use more of that?

Still, it requires effort to be a cultural alien. There are ingrained expectations that do not translate here—for example, any interest in efficiency. Sometimes things do work efficiently, but this is a country where time is abundant and money is scarce. For most, there is little connection between them.

In the small village grocery store, I stand in the vicinity of the woman who takes the money, which might be called the checkout line if there were indeed a line. I balance a package of paper towels, four loose potatoes, and a bottle of pomegranate juice in my arms because I can't find a basket. I try to decipher a way to line up and pay. But people are helter-skelter every-where, carrying their groceries because the only counter is cluttered with the plastic bags that should be by the produce; no conveyor belt runs toward the cash register, because there is no cash register, only a tablet, a pencil, and a box; and when I want cheese, the woman has to climb over the crates behind her to get out from the counter, and all the time I am standing there I want to improve their system, but there is no system that I can see.

When efficiency hysteria comes over me, I mentally slap my face and take a deep breath. *Well, Carol, what difference does it make? Is efficiency the goal of life? Or is being happy and satisfied the point? Why does it matter how much time it takes? Time is not money in this world.*

If the door opens a crack, I can see the system. If I look at the grocery store in its microcosm of family, culture, and economics, it is there. Yaya, the owner, has a son who is doing his homework in the front of the store while she talks with the driver of the Coca-Cola truck. Her mother is manning the cash box, writing the list of items sold in pencil in a notebook. Her father is sitting by the cooler, peeling onions. The village doctor, dressed in shorts, is standing in front with a group of men, flossing his teeth. There is full employment, there is time with family, there is a community, there *is* a system. It is just one that we WEIRDs do not recognize because we are using only one measure: time equals money. And we are stressed.

I went to the small hotel in the village to say good-bye to two visiting Canadian women. I asked for them at the front desk.

"*Las gringas,*" I said.

The manager claimed there were no gringas.

"Blonde?" I said.

He shook his head.

"A taxi is coming to take them to the airport." I knew he must have called the taxi for them. I was running out of descriptors.

No, he shook his head. I began to hear the music from *The Twilight Zone*, when his face brightened.

"But, *señora,* could it be they are not gringas but Canadians?"

I asked Maricela, my Spanish teacher, if she thought that both Americans and Canadians are called "gringos."

"Doesn't 'gringo' mean 'the other inhabitants of North America, who do not speak Spanish'?" I say "other inhabitants" because Mexicans are also North Americans and fellow inhabitants of the continent called "America."

"Oh, no, Carolina," she said. "The word 'gringos' refers only to people from the United States." She hastily assured me that it was not a negative word.

"Yes, I use it, too. But how can you tell who is a Canadian and who is from the United States?" This was the part that made no sense.

"Ah, Carolina, *muy fácil*. The *estadounidenses* are very unhappy. They have too much stress. I see that when they sit down at *la taquería*. I can always tell them from the Canadians."

In San Miguel, I asked the same question. Yes, only *estadounidenses* are gringos; no, it is not a derogatory term; and yes, they can always tell the Canadians apart from people from the United States. One restaurant owner told us she could tell because "the Americans have a way of speaking that is"—she paused tactfully—"very forceful."

With our forcefulness and our focus on time and money, we might easily think that Mexico, our next-door neighbor, is poor because she drives an old car and wears humble clothing. It is easy to think that we are wealthy because we have more cash. But Mexico is a millionaire many times over. Her wealth is just in a different currency. Her ancient family built more pyramids than the Egyptians, and were precise astronomers and mathematicians with sophisticated medicine, libraries, and art. Right on our doorstep, we have an opportunity to learn from our neighbor because the memory and knowledge of that greatness are not gone. They course just under the skin, a beating bloodline of a rich history. Our neighbor has many things we do not. They may look like small things; they may look simple because they do not require money. But they are things we could appreciate, that we could learn from and use.

I will always be a gringa. I still have my sixteen-digit credit card number memorized, because, well, "wherever you go, there you are." And wherever I am, I might need it. I still read blog posts like "Getting Things Done!" "Nineteen Ways to Be More Productive!" "Make a Million and Live a Better Life!"—the cultural exhortations based on time and money that fly across the border into my e-mail, assuring me I can be richer, therefore happier, if I just buy this one thing, read this book, or take this training. I still occasionally want that seaweed body wrap with the Pacifica masque and mineral scrub, but I don't miss it. So many of my toxins have been naturally released. I still have not mastered swearing in Spanish, but I am getting a little more expressive in spitting out *pinche puto pendejo baboso.*

I will always be a gringa, but I am a gringa in love with Mexico. As in all love affairs, accommodating myself to my love has changed me. Sometimes, when I am standing juggling paper towels, potatoes, and a bottle of pomegranate juice, that door opens a crack and I see something more, something different.

I do.

Because, thank goodness, this is Mexico—and that's how it goes.

ACKNOWLEDGMENTS

As a writer coming from a completely different profession, the list of people who have given me their hand and pulled, sometimes while my heels were dug tenaciously into the dirt, are of a length resembling the Manhattan telephone directory. I will spare you that. Here are just a few.

I have had wonderful teachers of the craft of writing. Special thanks to Laura Fraser and Eva Hunter for teaching me many things, including how to think about structure and how much time it takes to really edit.

Thanks to Professor Joseph Henrich at the University of British Columbia for clarifying his team's work on the immutability of culture to me.

I am indebted to the many authors who, through their works, have taught me about Mexican history and culture:

Ron Austin, *Peregrino: A Pilgrim Journey into Catholic Mexico*

Kathryn S. Blair, *Forging a Nation: The Story of Mexico from the Aztecs to the Present*

Jorge G. Castañeda, *Mañana Forever?*

Boyé De Mente, *The Mexican Mind!: Understanding & Appreciating Mexican Culture!*

T. R. Fehrenbach, *Fire and Blood*

Enrique Florescano, *National Narratives in Mexico: A History*

Alan Riding, *Distant Neighbors: A Portrait of the Mexicans*

Earl Shorris, *The Life and Times of Mexico*

Any errors in my understanding of their marvelous insights are, of course, mine.

My Beta readers' comments were invaluable: Thank you to Ted Dillingham, Ronnie Weiner, Cindy Mc-Mullen, and Janet Dunnett, with special thanks to Kenia Velásquez, who not only made instructive comments in English but also corrected thousands of missing accent marks in my Spanish. My eternal gratitude goes to Kristen Masters, partner in proofreading and master of the written word.

My Saturday morning writers' group not only gave insightful critiques but also helped to keep me sane, no small feat. Terry Baldwin, Jim Knoch, Sharon Conklin, Carolyn Roberts, you are a "dream team" of fellow travelers on the writing path.

In addition to being a writing colleague, Jim Knoch is an outstanding photographer who had the perfect image that said, "This is Mexico." Thank you, Jim, for allowing me to use it on the cover. Thanks also to Julie Metz for her cover design work and to Jim House and Leigh Karsch for holding my hand.

To Brooke Warner at She Writes Press for her kind and patient guidance—working with nervous authors cannot be easy. To my editors, Annie Tucker and Stuart Horwitz, this is a such a better book for your efforts. Thanks for making it a pleasure to work with you.

So many people have encouraged me that it would be impossible to name them all, but a special thank you to Susan Page, a force of nature and the director of the San Miguel Writers' Conference, for her encouragement and for insisting that I finally finish.

To my family—my mother, who still has a copy of my first book, an explication of the legal value of harassment training on her coffee table; my children, Sean and Jessica, who never once said, "You are doing what?" and my father, from whom I learned the value of telling stories. I hope he would be proud.

To Magali and Juan Pablo and their families for their love and patience in working with *Los Gringos*.

And to my first reader: my husband, Robert, partner in life and participant in the journey called "This is Mexico." Who, when I said, "I think I'll write a novel" said, "Why don't you stick to something you know?" and who challenged, pushed, and supported me in so many ways, including listening to every essay, often multiple times.

What will we talk about over lunch now?

ABOUT THE AUTHOR

CAROL MERCHASIN is a recovering lawyer, trainer, public speaker, and former partner at a large law firm, as well as an author involved in a longtime relationship with Mexico. She fell in love with the language, people, and culture on her first trip south in 1983, and she moved to San Miguel de Allende in 2006. She is a keen observer, an experienced researcher, and an enthusiastic student of Mexican culture.

She has read her work often in San Miguel at the Literary Sala, at the PEN/Faulkner Reading Series, and at a variety of nonprofit fundraising events, to rave reviews from Mexicans, Americans, and Canadians alike. Her e-book, *How It Goes in Mexico: Essays from an Expatriate*, won eLit Gold Awards in both Essay/Creative Nonfiction and Travel Essay.

SELECTED TITLES FROM SHE WRITES PRESS

She Writes Press is an independent publishing company founded to
serve women writers everywhere.
Visit us at www.shewritespress.com.

Renewable: One Woman's Search for Simplicity, Faithfulness, and Hope by
Eileen Flanagan. $16.95, 978-1-63152-968-9. At age forty-nine,
Eileen Flanagan had an aching feeling that she wasn't living up to her
youthful ideals or potential, so she started trying to change the world
—and in doing so, she found the courage to change her life.

Peanut Butter and Naan: Stories of an American Mother in The Far East
by Jennifer Magnuson. $16.95, 978-1-63152-911-5. The hilarious
tale of what happened when Jennifer Magnuson moved her family of
seven from Nashville to India in an effort to shake things up—and
got more than she bargained for.

*Her Name Is Kaur: Sikh American Women Write About Love, Courage,
and Faith* edited by Meeta Kaur. $17.95, 978-1-938314-70-4. An eye-
opening, multifaceted collection of essays by Sikh American women
exploring the concept of love in the context of the modern landscape
and influences that shape their lives.

*Flip-Flops After Fifty: And Other Thoughts on Aging I Remembered to
Write Down* by Cindy Eastman. $16.95, 978-1-938314-68-1. A
collection of frank and funny essays about turning fifty—and all the
emotional ups and downs that come with it.

*Seasons Among the Vines:Life Lessons from the California Wine Country
and Paris*by Paula Moulton. $16.95, 978-1-938314-16-2. New advice
on wine making, tasting, and food pairing—along with a spirited
account of the author's experiences in Le Cordon Bleu's pilot wine
program—make this second edition even better than the first.

Seeing Red: A Woman's Quest for Truth, Power, and the Sacred by Lone
Morch. $16.95, 978-1-938314-12-4. One woman's journey over inner
and outer mountains—a quest that takes her to the holy Mt. Kailas in
Tibet, through a seven-year marriage, and into the arms of the fierce
goddess Kali, where she discovers her powerful, feminine self.